Object-Oriented
Software Development

Object-Oriented Software Development

A Practical Guide

Mark Lorenz

IBM Programming Systems

P T R Prentice Hall

Englewood Cliffs, New Jersey 07632

Library of Congress Cataloging-in-Publication Data

Lorenz, Mark.
    Object-oriented software development : a practical guide / Mark
Lorenz.
      p.   cm.
    Includes bibliographical references and index.
    ISBN 0-13-726928-5
    1. Computer software--Development. 2. Object-oriented
programming.   I. Title.
QA76.76.D47L67 1993
005.1'1--dc20   92-18566
                                                          CIP

Editorial/production supervision
  and interior design: *Brendan M. Stewart*
Prepress buyer: *Mary Elizabeth McCartney*
Manufacturing buyer: *Susan Brunke*
Acquisitions editor: *Paul Becker*

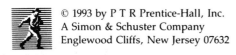 © 1993 by P T R Prentice-Hall, Inc.
A Simon & Schuster Company
Englewood Cliffs, New Jersey 07632

The publisher offers discounts on this book when ordered in bulk quantities. For more information, write: Special Sales/Professional Marketing, Prentice Hall, Professional Technical Reference Division, Englewood Cliffs, NJ 07632.

Printed in the United States of America
10 9 8 7 6 5 4 3 2

ISBN 0-13-726928-5

Prentice-Hall International (UK) Limited, *London*
Prentice-Hall of Australia Pty. Limited, *Sydney*
Prentice-Hall Canada Inc., *Toronto*
Prentice-Hall Hispanoamericana, S.A., *Mexico*
Prentice-Hall of India Private Limited, *New Delhi*
Prentice-Hall of Japan, Inc., *Tokyo*
Simon & Schuster Asia Pte. Ltd., *Singapore*
Editora Prentice-Hall do Brasil, Ltda., *Rio de Janeiro*

To Denise . . . for your love and support all these years,
and
Kelly . . . for reminding me of childhood's wonders.

I love you both.

Contents

Foreword

As the software industry gradually convinces itself of the benefits of switching to object-oriented methods and tools, developers and managers are asking some of the tough questions. They are willing to appreciate the power and elegance of object-oriented concepts, but they want to know how to apply these concepts in the day-to-day practice of software development: how to distribute tasks between team members, how to analyze and specify system requirements, how to approach testing, how to interface classes, what pitfalls to avoid in the process.

This book, the fourth in the Object-Oriented Series, provides a consistent set of answers to some of the most crucial problems of object-oriented software development. Through his own software development and his articles, Mark Lorenz has accumulated a considerable experience in object-orientedness. With this volume, he shares some of that experience with the reader, and provides a critical appraisal of the methodological advice offered by previous authors. The result should be of particular interest to software professionals who want to use object-oriented technology now, and to use it well.

Faithful to its title, Mark Lorenz's book is not a new theoretical contribution to the field but a practical guide for those who have decided to take the jump and apply object-oriented methods to real problems in industrial software development environments. Developers and managers alike will appreciate the matter-of-fact style, the chapter summaries, the case studies, the checklists, the illustrations, the precise definitions, the tool catalog of appendix B, and the many references to the literature. No doubt these features and others will cause many object-oriented practitioners to keep a copy of this book on their desks for frequent and easy reference.

—Bertrand Meyer

Preface

This book describes:

- An iterative development process.
- An object-oriented (O-O) development methodology.
- O-O software development phases.

The process described is primarily for managing O-O development efforts, and includes concerns such as scheduling and milestone completion.

The methodology described is a series of steps used to develop quality software. It focuses on objects in the user's world and how to accurately model them.

The phases set the framework for the entire effort. The phase descriptions include definitions of their prerequisites, activities, and deliverables.

The process and methodology documented here provide requirements for tools to support O-O development. The industry is severely lacking in tool support today. Most of the sections of this book can be supported reasonably well without on-line tools, through the use of CRC cards, for example.[1]

The information presented here is based on experiences of group development projects using O-O technology. Our teams benefited from working with industry leaders in O-O technology.

WHO SHOULD READ THIS BOOK

Managers of software development groups, business analysts, and software developers who are interested in learning how to develop software in a manner that directly models the user's business and adapts well to change will benefit from reading this book.

This is a *practitioner's* book, meant to help people whose job it is to develop and deliver software systems.

No prior knowledge of O-O concepts is required; however, this book does not attempt a rigorous tutorial of those concepts here. Readers should refer to the books and papers in Appendix A, "References" on page 111 for additional readings.

OBJECTIVES OF THIS BOOK

This book is intended to provide a process and methodology that can be followed to accomplish an analysis, design, implementation, and test of model objects for an application being developed. This book is geared toward the majority of software efforts: nontrivial functionality developed by a team of developers. Very small enhancements to existing code can certainly be developed without following every step discussed in this book—it is up to the development team's discretion to decide what to skip in that case.

The implementation language for the application being developed is assumed to be object oriented and the implementation environment is assumed to support message passing.

It is my intent to cover a broad spectrum of development topics at a moderate level of depth, as shown in Figure 1.

---

[1]CRC stands for "Class, Responsibilities, Collaborators." It is a technique that uses index cards, one per class, to document classes and "enact" system scenarios. The technique was originally proposed and used by Ward Cunningham and Kent Beck at Tektronix. See their article "A Laboratory for Teaching Object-Oriented Thinking," *SIGPLAN Notices*, vol. 24, (October 1989), p.10.

Topic Coverage

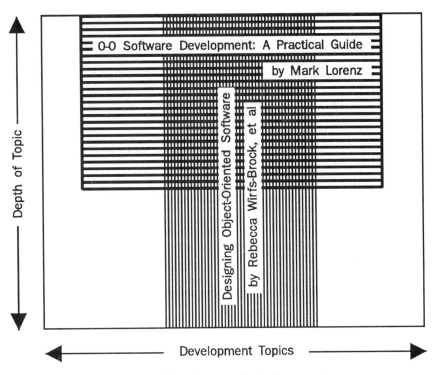

Figure 1.   Development Topic Coverage

There are books which work in a complimentary way with this book, filling in development "problem space" areas not covered as extensively in this book, but still compatible in the message and format. One such book is Rebecca Wirfs-Brock's book called *Designing Object-Oriented Software*. While there is overlap with the Wirfs-Brock book, this book fills a unique niche with a much-needed, start-to-finish guide to follow, including topics such as deliverables, team roles, and scheduling.

HOW THIS BOOK IS ORGANIZED

The book has the following sections:

CHAPTER 1: INTRODUCTION

An overview of where we've been and where we're going is presented. Concepts and terminology used in this book are explained.

CHAPTER 2: ITERATIVE DEVELOPMENT PROCESS

Details for managing the development process are described. This is split out separately to help with understanding the process.

CHAPTER 3: O-O DEVELOPMENT METHODOLOGY

The steps to develop an application are described, from finding the right objects to testing. The steps include the tool requirements necessary to support the individual steps.

An Automated Teller Machine (ATM) application is used in examples throughout the book.[2]

CHAPTER 4: SOFTWARE DEVELOPMENT PHASES

The characteristics of the phases are described, including their uses of the process and methodology. Prerequisites, activities, and deliverables for each phase are described.

---

[2]The ATM application has been used as a sample application by my group since early 1988. It was chosen due to the fact that it is well understood, of moderate complexity, and a real business application. It is therefore not surprising that the Wirfs-Brock book has coincidentally included a similar application, with a somewhat different solution. This should serve to make the two books more useful to readers.

CHAPTER 5: PUTTING IT ALL TOGETHER

This chapter recaps how the development phases, process, and methodology relate to each other. Integration with existing systems and tips on getting started are presented.

THE APPENDICES

The appendices give supplemental in-depth information for further reading on a variety of topics, such as how to organize your team, line item scheduling, estimating, and coding standards.

A couple of general comments about the book:

1. The terminology used throughout this book is also used in Smalltalk. Other terms are perfectly acceptable as well, but are not included for simplicity. For example, *member function* (C++ corresponds to *method* as used in this book. Terms are defined in a glossary at the back.

2. The delivery vehicle for the information being developed throughout this book can be on index cards, typed into a computer with a vanilla text editor, entered into object-oriented analysis and design tools, or other. The way of presenting the information content is not meant to imply a required way of documenting the analysis and design information, but is merely a means of communicating the types of information that needs to be kept.

This book was born of a need . . . a need for guidelines to follow for deliverables, team roles, and scheduling on an O-O project. One of the first O-O projects I was on began in early 1988 with a team of 6 IBMers and a couple of contractors. We were using Smalltalk/V286 under DOS, and later Smalltalk/V PM under OS/2. We had essentially no tools other than those provided by the Smalltalk environment. We had no previous experience to tell us how to schedule iterations, what deliverables to create, etc. What we did know was what we wanted to do. And what we believed was that O-O was the way to do it.

Three years later, looking back on one project and seeing other spin-offs from it, I decided to take pen to paper (keyboard to bits?) and document guidelines that others could follow, based on my experience as a technical lead on an O-O effort. It was a bigger task than I originally envisioned, with this book as the result.

A lot of what is written here is based on practical use. Some of what is here exists to "fill in the gaps" of what we *should* have done, if we had had the hindsight to help us out at the time. Groups at IBM, including my own, are now using this next iteration in our current efforts.

I hope that this book lives up to its name and thereby helps move the industry toward successful use of object technology.

—*Mark Lorenz*

ACKNOWLEDGMENTS

I owe a special thanks to John Manifold for helping to work through what was really happening (or *should* happen) during the phases of development. Thanks John! I also owe a special thanks to Kevin Haga for his help in understanding the issues of how testing fits into an iterative development process.

I would like to thank all those providing review comments for helping me to create the best book possible. I would especially like to thank Bill Haynes for his original work in documenting the iterative development process that we were following on our project at the time. I would also like to thank Tim Wilson for his comments on testing as it relates to O-O development. Corny as it may sound, I'd like to thank IBM for providing me the opportunity to become addicted to object technology—I hope to pay the investment back in spades.

I'd also like to mention a few of the many great O-O people I've had the privilege to work with over the years: Bob Brodd, Kathy Carroll, Jeff Kidd, Al Davis, Bill Felton, Hayden Lindsey, and Pete Dimitrios. Thanks to you and everyone else involved for making the project fun as well as successful.

Finally, I must thank Jeff McKenna—certainly for his review comments, but even more importantly for his inspiration, enthusiasm, insights, and example of what it means to "think *objec*tively". Thanks for being the catalyst in many design "reactions" that moved the project forward!

ABOUT THE AUTHOR

Mark Lorenz is a veteran of software development, having worked on a variety of software and hardware configurations, methodologies, team sizes, and companies since 1977. He has been concentrating on developing products using object technology since 1987. Mark has articles appearing in publications such as the *Journal of Object-Oriented Programming* and the *Hotline on Object-Oriented Technology*, and has appeared on panels in conferences such as *ObjectWorld*. He currently works for IBM in Cary, NC.

TRADEMARKS

Smalltalk/V is a registered trademark of Digitalk, Inc.

Envy is a trademark of Object Technology International, Inc.

ParcPlace, Smalltalk-80, and Objectworks are registered trademarks of ParcPlace Systems, Inc.

Rational is a registered trademark and Rational Rose is a trademark of Rational.

Instantiations and Application Organizer Plus are trademarks of Instantiations, Inc.

OpenWindows and SPARC are trademarks of Sun Microsystems, Inc.

OSF/Motif is a trademark of Open Software Foundation, Inc.

OS/2 is a trademark of International Business Machines Corporation.

RISC System/6000 is a trademark of International Business Machines Corporation.

ObjectMaker is a registered trademark of Mark V Systems Limited.

Prograph is a trademark of The Gunakara Sun Systems, Ltd.

Profile/V is a trademark of First Class Software.

OOATool is a trademark of Object International.

AM/ST is a registered trademark of SoftPert Systems, Ltd.

ObjectOry is a trademark of Objective Systems.

Nexpert Object is a trademark of Neuron Data Inc.

VERSANT is a registered trademark of Versant Object Technology Corporation.

GemStone is a registered trademark of Servio Corporation.

Tigre Programming Environment is a trademark of Tigre Object Systems, Inc.

Other product names may be trademarks of their respective companies.

Object-Oriented
Software Development

Chapter 1

Introduction

"When it is not necessary to make a decision, it is necessary not to make a decision."

Lord Falkland

A large part of what is presented here is geared toward providing a way to put off making decisions about complex systems that we don't understand until we understand what we're talking about better.

Before we jump headlong into detailed discussions of the process, methodology, and phases, let's take a brief look at where we've been and where we're going and define some basic terms as used in this book.

1.1 A SAMPLE APPLICATION

The application developed in the examples in this book is an Automated Teller Machine (ATM) banking application.[1] It was chosen because it is small enough to cover reasonably well in a book this size (please pardon the simplifying assumptions I have made) and is well

---

[1] A suggested exercise is described in Appendix K, "An Exercise for the Reader" if you'd like to develop an application along with the ATM application that is developed in the text. You can certainly develop a moderately-sized problem of your own also.

understood by most people. The assumption is that banks do not have an ATM capability but perceive market demand for better services. "Our" bank then decides to pursue an ATM application development, using the process and methodology detailed in this book.

We are going to assume that the initial requirements stated by the users of the system to the system analysts were:

ATM CUSTOMER REQUIREMENTS DRAFT

1. 24-hour access to:
    a. Access savings and checking accounts
    b. Move money between accounts
    c. Withdraw cash
        1) Default amount
        2) Specified amount
    d. Deposit money to an account
    e. Get an account balance
2. Log transactions
3. Cancel a transaction at any time before it is submitted
4. Failure security
    a. Card kept if too many invalid attempts
5. Multiple transactions for a single access
6. Business policies
    a. $200/day withdrawal limit

1.2 THE TRADITIONAL APPROACH

For the past 15 years or so, the most widely accepted way to develop software has been the *waterfall process* and *structured methodology*.[2] In order to better understand where we're going, let's take a look at where we've been.

The *waterfall process* for software development is shown in Figure 1.1. The activities flow primarily in one direction, building the system in a monolithic fashion.

The process has reviews at the end of each phase, where the deliverables are agreed to and put under change control. Decisions made

---

[2]The waterfall process and structured methodology do not have to be used together. The problems traditionally encountered can be attributed to one or the other or both. Also, an iterative process can certainly be used with a functional decomposition methodology—*but* there are factors such as encapsulation that make iterations easier to deal with in an O-O system.

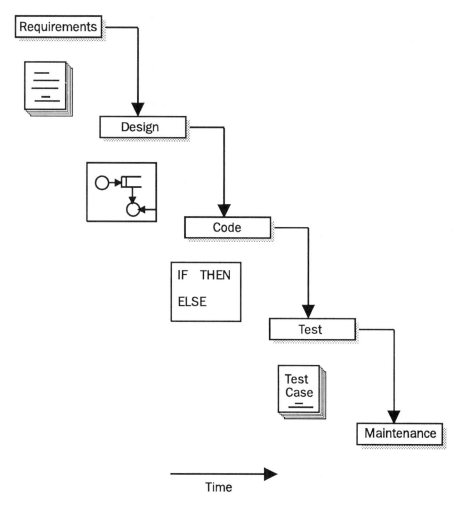

Figure 1.1   The Waterfall Process

downstream are based on the earlier deliverables. Activities are primarily concentrated on one type of work, whether requirements documentation, dataflow diagram (DFD) development, coding, or testing. The test group bases its work on the requirements documented at the start. The development group (separately) designs and codes the system.

1.2.1 Structured Methodology Overview

A structured methodology is a top-down functional decomposition of the system, as it is understood. In a structured methodology, the developer works with *dataflow diagrams* (DFDs) and *structure charts*, both of which focus on *processes* (functions) and *data* being passed between the processes (where the data come to rest is called a datastore). This methodology was developed as a means to emulate the system being developed by translating it from *human* (user) terms and concepts into *computer* terms and concepts. So, the customer's real-world objects, such as *customers, accounts,* and *transactions,* are not carried over to the application implementation (other than in the user interface). Instead, the implementation has computer processes, such as *accept user input, calculate withholding,* and *enqueue token.*

1.2.2 A Structured Methodology Solution

Let's use our ATM application as a vehicle to examine the structured methodology in greater detail. I will not go into much depth on the structured techniques for developing software, but there are a number of books available on the topic. I would recommend reading Tom DeMarco's book *Structured Analysis and System Specification* (Prentice Hall, Englewood Cliffs, NJ, 1979) for a complete discussion of structured techniques.

1.2.2.1 The development team

In a structured methodology, the developer initially focuses on the *data* that are flowing between computer *processes* that manipulate those data. The developer documents these flows on a *dataflow diagram* (DFD).[3] Figure 1.2 shows a DFD for the ATM application.

This DFD would be broken down further, in layers of more detail, until a description of any process could be written within one page of pseudo-code. Pseudo-code is nothing more than English prose written within some loose conventions. For example, pseudo-code for the *Display Account Balance* process might be:

PSEUDO-CODE FOR DISPLAY
ACCOUNT BALANCE **PROCESS**

For each record in the Account File,
  If the account number = the number to update,
    Return the account balance field.
  End if.
End for.
Return an indication that the record was not found.

---

[3]Some methodologies advocate the use of modified structured techniques in O-O development. I disagree with this approach. It is too much a case of a "round peg

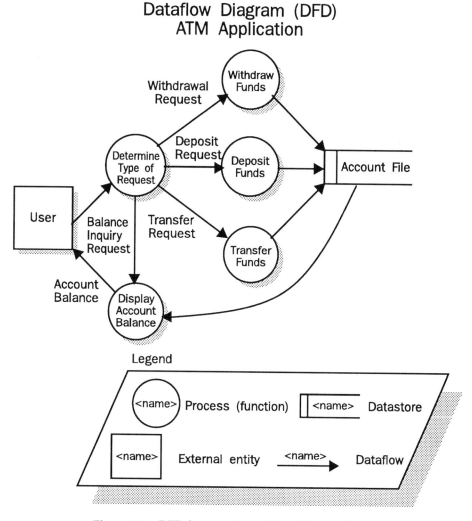

Figure 1.2   DFD for a portion of the ATM Application

So, pseudo-code is a "structured English" that parallels but contains less details than the final code.

Each flow and datastore (where data come to rest) would be documented in a *Data Dictionary*, which would show its exact contents.

The DFD is the logical layout of the application from the analysis of what it should do, but it does *not* contain control information

---

in a square hole." Having developed large systems using DFDs, I would find it difficult to use DFDs to model an application in objects. The focus of the paradigms is too different. It's not that it can't be done, just as I can use a screwdriver handle to drive in a nail . . . it's more a case of "why would you want to?"

or a structure for how to put it together at implementation time. That is where *structure charts* come in. After the DFD has been done, a *structure chart* is created to show more details of how the application is to be put together into something that will run on a computer. Figure 1.3 is a structure chart for the *Balance Inquiry* portion of the ATM application.

This hierarchical diagram shows what processes call other processes and what the parameters are, including control and data.

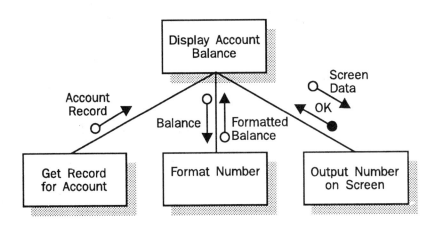

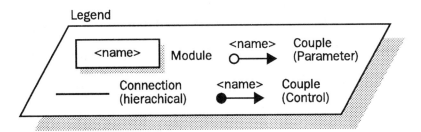

Figure 1.3   Structure Chart for a Portion of the ATM Application

At this point, the coding can begin, based on the DFDs, structure charts, and pseudo-code. Once code has been written, the test team can start running function tests against the code and the usability team can start looking at the user interface.[4] And . . . the users can start seeing what they're going to get—which may or may not be what they thought they were getting or what they need to solve their problems.

Finally, the system is delivered and put into production.

1.2.2.2 The database team

In parallel with the development team using DFDs and structure charts to model the computer processes, flows, and structure, another team is worrying about how the data are stored and accessed. These people use entity-relationship (E/R) diagrams to document their data models. Figure 1.4 shows an E/R diagram for the ATM application.

The focus is on how to efficiently store the application information into a database (DB), such as a relational DB. This team creates the necessary tables to enable the application. The development team uses these tables in writing the application code. The tables in a relational DB are set up to meet computer implementation requirements, such as minimizing the update problems by ensuring little duplication of the same data in multiple tables.

1.2.2.3 The test team

While the development team is designing and starting to code the system, the test team is using the requirements and design documents to write test cases. When the pieces of code are delivered, the test cases must be modified to match the reality that evolved from changes that took place in the interim.

1.3 WHY CHANGE?

What's wrong with the waterfall process and structured methodologies for developing software?

There are some basic assumptions in a traditional approach to development that make it very difficult to succeed in today's world of complex systems:

---

[4]Granted, for a larger application, documentation of what the user interface may look like could have been done earlier—but this is the first time to actually get your hands on running system code.

Entity-Relationship (E/R) Diagram
ATM Application

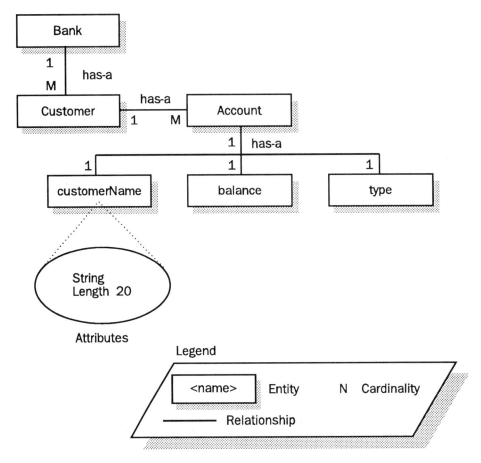

Figure 1.4 E/R Diagram for a Portion of the ATM Application

• *No change*

It is inherent in the lock-step cascading of the steps in a waterfall process that work that has gone before is still correct. Unfortunately, the customer's requirements, competitive products, and understanding of the problem *change* over time. The traditional approaches do not plan for this change, nor do they facilitate it when it happens. Instead, the unplanned changes ripple through the system's architecture, documentation, and code, with no time allowed for this sometimes massive impact.

The iterative development process (IDP) and O-O methodology described in this book *plan* for change.

• *Perfect understanding*

Since the waterfall approach attempts to design a system all at once up front, followed by a monolithic implementation, the assumption is that the system is perfectly understood during the initial stages. It is very difficult for humans to understand a complex system well.

Another aspect of understanding is communication. English is an ambiguous language, with many interpretations. Requirements documents and design specifications are written in this ambiguous language. In addition, functionally-decomposed systems make it difficult for users to understand the system. So, users who *thought* they knew what they were asking for don't recognize or need what they get when the system is delivered.[5] The user's effective involvement, through techniques such as an analysis prototype described in this book, help ensure that this doesn't happen in future development efforts.

The traditional approaches to software development do not consistently deliver products on time and within cost. In fact, only 1 percent of large software systems are delivered on time and within cost.[6] The process and methodology described in this book attempt to address the problems of the waterfall and structured approaches.

1.4 OVERVIEW OF WHERE WE'RE GOING

The topics covered in this book, namely the iterative development process, object-oriented development methodology, and software development phases, are interrelated in the complex world of software development. The major topics are embedded, one within another, as shown in Figure 1.5.

The *development phases* form the framework of the entire effort. They define the prerequisites, activities, and deliverables for different sets of efforts in developing software. The main focus of the book is on the *analysis* and *design and test* phases. These are where the main software development efforts take place. The *business* and *packaging*

---

[5]Not all differences and benefits of object-oriented and iterative development are detailed here. For example, another benefit of O-O is that the user's terms carry forward all the way to the code (this is called real-world modeling), so that the likelihood of effective communication is greater.

[6]Richard P. Gabriel, "Solving the Software Crisis," *Unix Review*, vol. 9, 7, (July 1991), 27.

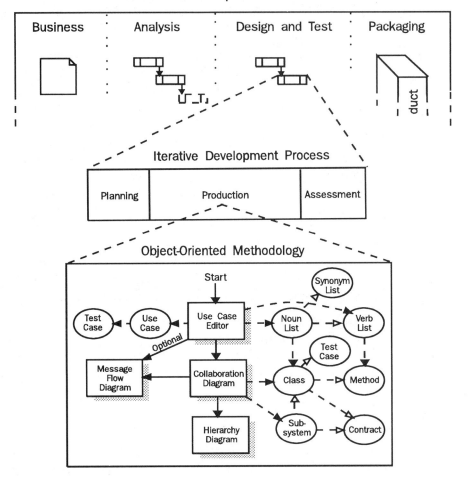

Figure 1.5 Development Phases, Process, and Methodology

phases are discussed primarily in light of their deliverables and pre-requisites, respectively, as they relate to the software development phases.

The *iterative development process* (IDP) defines the steps to manage the development efforts. This process is used within the analysis and design and test phases, when the software is being built. As the name implies, the IDP is iterative in nature, with repeating *periods* of types of efforts. The output of one iteration is the input for the next.

The *object-oriented development methodology* defines the steps in developing quality O-O software. The methodology is used within the production portion of the IDP.

In order to most effectively present the material, building understanding as we go, I am going to present these pieces of the software puzzle inside out. So, we discuss the process and methodology in generic terms first. Then, we talk about the phases in specifics, detailing how the process and methodology are used. Finally, we put the pieces together, revisiting this discussion as well as dealing with integration, maintenance, and startup issues.

I have tried to make each section of the document stand on its own, so that the reader may choose the best order for his or her needs.

1.5 CONCEPTS

The following sections present basic introductory terms that provide a fundamental foundation for further discussions. Additional terms and concepts are described as they are introduced.

1.5.1 Process Concepts

This section provides a basic understanding of the meaning of the development process terms used in this book.

CONCEPT	MEANING
Analysis	Analysis is the portion of the software development effort that focuses on the problem (or business) domain. The primary product of this effort is a clear, complete, verified, well-understood statement of the system requirements. The key classes of objects for the problem domain are also identified, with the user's vocabulary captured in nouns (classes) and verbs (methods).
Design	Design is the portion of the software development effort that focuses on the solution domain. The primary product of this effort is a software system that accurately models the portion of the business being automated.
Iteration	An iteration is a single development cycle of a part of the system. It is the major component of the Iterative Development Process (IDP). An iteration is generally a multi-month effort to work on a set of product line items. A single line item might be worked on multiple times during multiple iterations.

1.5.2 O-O Concepts

This section provides a basic understanding of the meaning of the object-oriented terms used in this book. It is not the intent of this book to cover in great detail all aspects of object-oriented concepts. The reader is referred to Appendix A for a list of references that go into more depth in this area.

CONCEPT	**MEANING**
Object	An object is the basis for all other object-oriented concepts. In its simplest form, an object is anything that models "things" in the real world. These "things" may be physical entities such as cars, or events such as a concert, or abstractions such as a general-purpose account.
	When discussing an object, there are often two possible meanings: a class or an instance. In this book, an object refers to an instance.
Class	A class is a template that defines the structure and capabilities of an object instance. The class definition includes the state data and the behaviors (methods) for the instances of that class. The class can be thought of as a factory, creating instances as needed. For example, an *Account* class may have methods to allow deposits and withdrawals to be made, using a *balance* instance variable to hold the current balance. This definition defines how an account works, but it is not an actual account.
Instance	An instance (or just "object") is an actual object, waiting to perform services and holding some state data. For example, a person's account at a bank is an instance of the Account class. It is possible to make deposits and withdrawals, or possibly to ask the account for its current balance. This account shares information (such as methods) with all instances of the same class, but they are different objects, with separate state data (such as their balances).
Message	Objects communicate via messages. In order to request a service from another object, an object sends it a message. This is the only means to get information from an object, since its data are not directly accessible (this is called encapsulation).

Method   A class service or behavior. Methods are exe-
                                    cuted whenever an object receives a message.
                                    They contain the logic, in the form of more mes-
                                    sage sends, for the objects in a class.

Inheritance   You can organize similar types of classes into
                                    categories called class hierarchies. The lower-
                                    level classes (called subclasses) can use the ser-
                                    vices of all the higher classes in their hierarchy.
                                    This is called *inheritance*. Inheritance is simply a
                                    way of reusing services and data.

                                         You can significantly increase your produc-
                                    tivity by finding ways to reuse existing classes.
                                    Inheritance is one of these ways. For example, a
                                    SavingsAccount is a type of general *Account,* and
                                    an *IRAAccount* is a type of *SavingsAccount,* as
                                    shown in Figure 1.6. The *SavingsAccount* inher-
                                    its the capability to handle deposits from the *Ac-
                                    count* class.

Dynamic binding   Dynamic binding, also known as *late* binding,
                                    associates a variable with an object class *during*

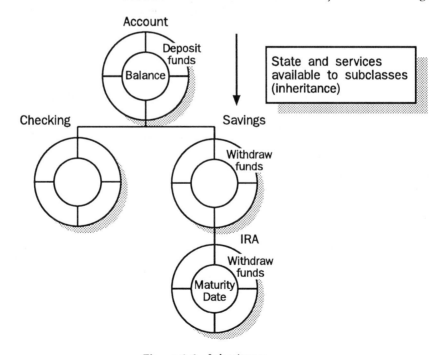

Figure 1.6 Inheritance

the system's execution. This allows the system to dynamically decide what method to use, based on the type of object being dealt with. For example, the *SavingsAccount* and *CdAccount* classes may both have a withdraw method, since the bank has different withdrawal policies for the types of accounts. Using dynamic binding (and polymorphism), the system would choose the right method code to execute.

Static binding

Static binding, also known as *early* binding, associates a variable with an object class *at compile time.* This allows the system to decide what method to use, based on the type of object *declared* as being dealt with.

Polymorphism

Polymorphism is the capability of a single variable to refer to different objects that fulfill certain message protocol responsibilities (roles). For example, an instance variable called *account* can hold a *SavingsAccount* or *IraAccount* object at different times (see Figure 1.7). No matter which type of object the variable holds at a given time, it can be sent a *withdraw funds* message.

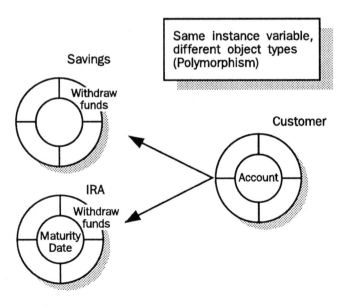

Figure 1.7   Polymorphism

Polymorphism, along with dynamic binding, make type-specific coding, such as an *iraWithdraw funds* message, unnecessary.

Encapsulation

Encapsulation has to do with information hiding. In object-oriented systems, you cannot directly access an object's state data, but must ask the object for services, which may include returning a piece of the data.[7] There are a variety of reasons for keeping objects "black boxes" (hiding the internal workings), but the primary one is to minimize ripples caused by maintenance changes. After all, client code shouldn't care how a service is provided—only that the desired result occurs.

Application

An application in an O-O system is a collection of classes that work together to provide some related functionality to the end user. In the ATM sample application in this book, we will see what classes are part of the application and how they work together to give the bank customers the functionality they require.

As Figure 1.8 shows, an application utilizes classes from various places in the inheritance

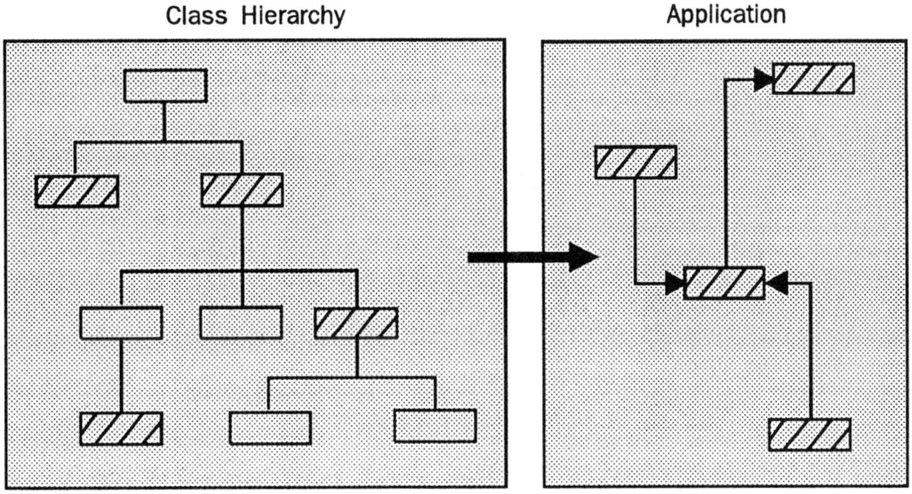

Class Hierarchy   **Application**

Figure 1.8 Class Hierarchy versus O-O Application

---

[7]Some languages, such as C++, allow you to break an object's encapsulation, but this is not recommended.

hierarchy. The classes are not necessarily related via inheritance. They send each other messages to collaborate on the task at hand.

1.6 SUMMARY

Traditional approaches to software development, namely top-down functional decomposition within a waterfall process, do not consistently deliver systems on time and under budget. This is largely due to the fact that this approach does not plan for change and does not facilitate modeling the more complicated applications in today's world.

The object-oriented approach described in this book addresses the shortcomings of previous approaches, by utilizing a new development framework, an iterative development process (IDP), and a methodology that models real-world objects in the application.

Chapter 2

Iterative Development Process

"The closer I get to my goal, the better my chance of discovering what it is."

Ashleigh Brilliant

The Iterative Development Process (IDP) is the framework for laying out activities for different time periods in the analysis and design and test development phases. The IDP is a technique that manages complexity and plans for change during software development. It is a *framework* around the methodology steps used in developing and documenting the software itself. The IDP is used during two of the four phases of development described in Chapter 4, "Software Development Phases."

The goals of the IDP are:

1. To ensure the flexibility to build the *right* system by systematically verifying and refining requirements with customers at planned intervals.
2. To allow detailed plans to build complex systems that more closely match reality, by staging a rollout of the functions as more of the system is understood.

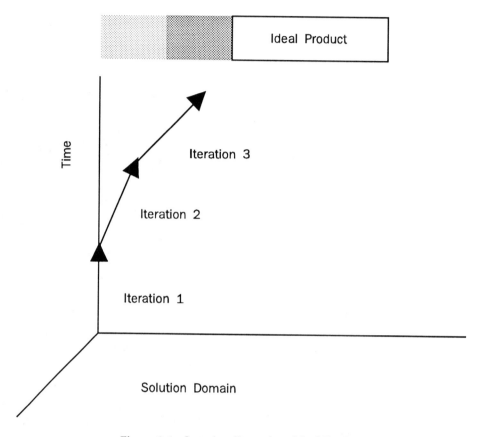

Figure 2.1   Iterating Toward an Ideal Product

Figure 2.1 depicts the main goal behind the IDP: to more closely follow the changing reality of the "ideal" product that meets our requirements.[1]

2.1 THE PROCESS

There is no single "correct" usage of the iterative process—the number of iterations and their duration depend on the system being developed. Some rules of thumb are presented here as guidelines. These

---

[1]The chart is adapted from Mark Lorenz, "Getting started with object technology: effectively planning for change," *Hotline on Object-Oriented Technology,* vol. 2, no. 11 (September 1991), p. 10.

rules of thumb are based on team experiences from doing O-O and non-O-O development for a number of years. Your company should keep statistics on actual experiences to provide better guidelines on future projects.

The IDP must remain a *controlled* process. Be careful not to "waltz through the solution space" while you are using the IDP. The IDP does not imply that you should just keep iterating as long as you have "more to do." You need to make sure that you remain *requirements driven,* using the requirements as the basis for completion. It is important that management ensures that the iterations converge on the verified requirements.

The Iterative Development Process (IDP) is depicted in Figure 2.2 and is described in the following sections.

2.1.1 An Iteration

A single iteration consists of a planning, production, and assessment period (see Figure 2.2). The iterations discussed here are major iterations of the system or a subsystem. There are numerous build iterations that occur during each major iteration. These build cycle iterations are discussed in Appendix G, "Build Cycle."

Iterative development is not incremental development. In *iterative* development, the same portion of the system is worked on a number of times, possibly rewriting it largely from scratch based on increased understanding of the task and related requirements. While it is true that you are incrementally adding function to your evolving system with each iteration, you will need to iterate on complex or ill-defined portions of the system a number of times.

Another misconception is that *one* iteration across the system is iterative development—it is not. While some portion(s) of the system may only need one iteration, it should not be the case that the whole system only needs one. This is another case of an incremental delivery.

2.1.1.1 Planning

The planning period starts an iteration. It is used to adapt to changing requirements, resources, schedules, and prerelease "driver" code contents. The activities consist of:

1. *Update and prioritize system requirements.*

    Update the requirements specification, separating requirements by release. As you clarify requirements with your users, capture the new insights in the documentation, along with the reasoning behind the decisions.

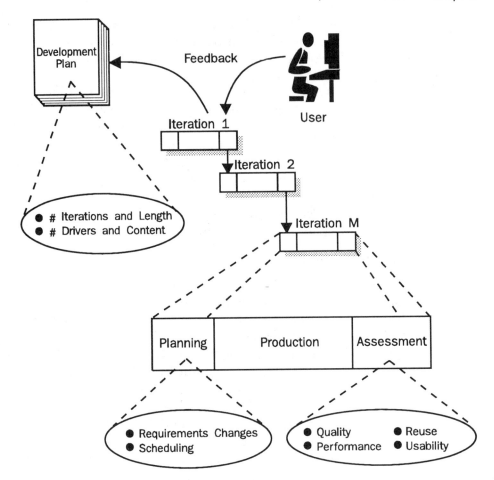

Figure 2.2   Iterative Development Process

2. *Document external dependencies and deliverables.*

   The ideal situation is to have no dependencies. The norm, of course, is to have many. Take the time and effort to list everything that you have assumed others will provide, whether other product code, documentation, equipment for your people, or training. Make sure everyone is clear on the items . . . and then do your best to work as independently as you can, so that when they slip, you may not have to.

3. *Determine specific goals for each iteration.*

   Having logical groups of functionality available at one time facilitates user involvement and usability testing, as well as the side benefit of allowing the developers to have a partially usable system to exercise in their daily tasks. For example, an iteration goal could be "The system components will all work together" or "The xyz functionality will be completed."

4. *Establish a schedule.*

Remember that there are minor iterations within a major iteration. Complex line items should have schedule plans for multiple iterations.

Relationships to requirements should be maintained, so that requirements can be tracked to current line items.

Appendix H, "Sample Line Item Schedule and Description," shows an example of line items and schedule for an iteration. H.1, "Estimating" talks about estimating the amount of effort to come up with the schedule.

Be careful not to plan too much—you'll fall into the waterfall approach trap. Plan for what you know; discover as you go.

2.1.1.2 Production

The production period is when the analysis, design, and implementation of the iteration line items occur. The movement through the activities for a single line item is rapid and follows a general pattern, as described in Appendix G, "Build cycle." The emphasis on reuse, quality, and performance will depend on the phase of development and are discussed in subsequent chapters of this book.

During the production period, the O-O methodology described in Chapter 3, "O-O Development Methodology," is followed to produce the line item software. This methodology describes the deliverables for the software. During the design and test phase, the test team will be taking builds to provide quick feedback to the developers and to iterate on the system test cases. See Section 4.3.2, "Test Overview."

2.1.1.3 Assessment

The assessment completes the iteration. It is used to evaluate the system according to a variety of criteria[2]:

1. *Conformance to customer requirements*

Does it do and *only* do what the customers require? In this type of dynamic environment, it is especially important to keep a close eye out for "feature creep," where developers put in "simple" enhancements that cause unnecessary work.

---

[2]These criteria were originally documented by Jeff Barnett et al., *Iterative Development Process Guide*, IBM 11000 Regency Pkwy., Cary, NC, Draft 1, June 27, 1990.

2. *Usability*

Can users accomplish their goals? Can they find the actions they want to take? Are the most used actions most readily available? Are the terms meaningful to the users?

3. *Competitiveness*

Does the level of function meet or exceed the levels of function in competitive products of similar price? If you don't know who your competition is or what their products are like, you can't be sure your product will be competitive. It is essential that your planners and developers are aware of the state of the art.

4. *Performance*

Is the performance acceptable? Remember that the definition of what is acceptable is tempered by the purpose of the code. For example, if the code is throwaway it does not need to meet production performance criteria.

5. *Extensibility*

How easy is it to add new functionality?

6. *Reusability*

Have abstractions been created? Abstraction has to do with pulling out common characteristics of a group of classes into a new higher-level class so that sharing can occur. For example, if you decided that, for your bank, you had checking, savings, and CD accounts with no abstract *Account* class, you would end up duplicating a lot of methods having to do with managing the accounts, such as *deposit* and *withdraw*. In addition, the abstractions themselves may replace a *number* of classes. For example, a *String* class may replace classes such as *customerName*, *accountType*, and *statusMessage*, which are really just *instances* of a string. The volume of classes (and code) will be significantly higher, with no added function, if abstractions are not used.

Are methods doing only one thing? Smaller, single-minded methods are more reusable. Are responsibilities with the right classes? A good fit increases the likelihood that future subclasses will be able to reuse the services. Are input parameters being wisely used? Different flavors of services with different sets of parameters may be desirable (reusing each other!). Are user exits available in the design? An example of a user exit might be passing a block of code to execute to a sort routine, so that new types of objects can be sorted.

Has the company's reuse library been enhanced by the project? Every project has some area of expertise that can be captured to add new components to the company's assets in the re-use library.

7. *Reliability*

Is the code robust enough for its purpose? Is the mean time between failures acceptable? Again, code to be used for prototype demonstrations versus code for the space shuttle's life-support systems have different degrees of acceptability.

The primary means of assessing the product under development according to these criteria are through:

1. *Customer reviews*

The importance of customer involvement cannot be over-emphasized. Validation and updating of requirements and verification of design necessitate involvement of customers. Customer reviews should be scheduled during the assessment period of each major iteration.

2. *Extensive internal use of the system*

Different groups in the organization should exercise the pre-release "driver" code, including usability, test, information development, and software development groups.

It is useful to have members of the development team cycle through testing of the system. This has the dual benefit of:
   a. Finding, documenting, and resolving bugs in the system.
   b. Educating the development members on the entire system.
Development team members tend to cloister themselves in their own part of the system, never to venture into other areas. It is important during their development that they have some understanding of the "bigger picture." If possible, you should consider having your developers and testers work in the users' area, so that they are forced to *use* the application they're developing and understand the users' job.

The full system's code should be used as much as possible during assessment, unit testing, and function testing. It is important to *use* the code in many situations by many people, since this is the *only* effective way to achieve truly robust code.

3. *Design reviews*

Your development team can look for abstractions, collaboration, and responsibilities to see if reuse is facilitated.

4. *Competitive assessment group evaluation*

If your company has a competitive assessment group that is responsible for keeping abreast of the latest developments in the marketplace, it could provide inputs as to how the product under development compares to other products.

QUALITY MEASUREMENT: It is important to have tools in place to capture detailed statistical information during the development process, especially the assessment phase, to facilitate performing ongoing causal analysis to improve the process and product. A problem reporting system that has granularity at least to the class level is needed. Problem types range from *does not meet requirements* to *crashes the system*. By tracking defects to a particular class, the product and reuse library can be made more robust.

Different actions can result from analyzing the statistics you collect. For example, looking at classes that have a lot of bugs reported against them can indicate a need for a rewrite or indicate the need for another class, if that one is being used improperly due to an unmet need. See Appendix I, "Measurements and Metrics," for further discussions of measurements, metrics, and how they're used.

During the assessment period (see Figure 2.3), the details of the development process itself should be examined to see if there are defects being injected due to[3]:

1. Poor communications

    Tools, conferencing forums, expertise availability, focal points, and meetings may be needed.

2. Lack of education

    Mentors, local classes, different staffing mixes, and career "blueprints" may address these problems.

3. Oversight

    Reduction of interruptions, tools, reviews, and process streamlining will reduce these types of errors.

4. Transcription

    Breakup of tedious tasks, tool automation, and reduced interruptions are geared toward helping reduce transcription errors.

5. Process problems

    Automation of steps, process flexibility, and reduction of steps will help.

Try to foster the view of causal analysis as part of the team's goal of constant improvement, and not as a personal attack. This will not always be easy, since developers naturally take pride of ownership in

---

[3]These points and the related figure are adapted from the *Defect Prevention Process* course from the IBM Quality Institute, Thornwood, NY.

The Defect-Prevention Process

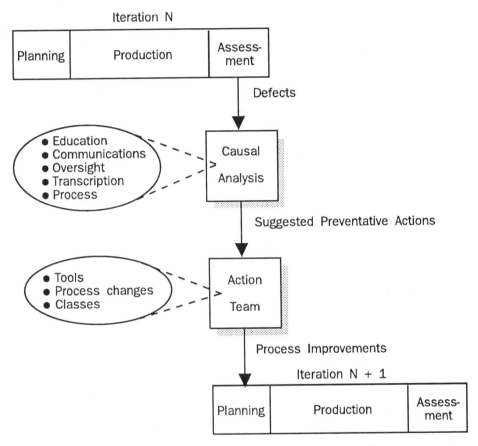

Figure 2.3 Causal Analysis and the IDP Assessment Period

"their" classes. A positive, constructive attitude is needed in this situation.

2.1.2 The Number of Iterations

The number of major iterations depends on the application being developed. A rule of thumb is that there will typically be three to six iterations on a system of moderate size and complexity (around 200 classes and 3,000 methods). This typically results in seven to eighteen months *development* time for a release (add system test and packaging time). Factors affecting the number of iterations include:

1. The size of the project.

    A larger project will certainly require more iterations, since it is important that the length of any one iteration is not too long.

2. The stability of the requirements.

    A project with many unknowns will need more iterations to firm up the requirements.

3. The complexity of the system.

    A complex (sub)system will require more iterations to explore and develop its functions.

4. The productivity of the people and environment.

    Lack of support tools will require a number of line items and iterations *in addition* to the product's line items to develop these tools. Lack of appropriate skill levels in the team members will require additional iterations to come up with a good design.

Of course, within these major iterations, there are minor build cycle iterations during production (see Appendix G, "Build Cycle").

2.1.3 The Duration of Iterations

The duration of the major iterations depends on the "chunks" of effort that are to be attempted at any one cycle. The duration of the iterations can certainly vary from one to another. Typically, an iteration will be around 3 ½ months long. For this typical iteration cycle, two weeks may be spent in planning, two to three weeks in assessment, and around 2 ½ months in production. It is suggested that an iteration should not be longer than three to four months, since this runs counter to the goals of iterating in the first place: customer involvement in the process for requirement clarification, and schedule rollout for complexity management.

Factors affecting the duration of iterations:

1. The logical "chunks" of function that are delivered.

    Some amount of functionality just naturally "goes together." Any less and the functions would be difficult to use or would appear incomplete.

2. The availability of customers.

    The assessment period requires involvement of the customers.

3. The volatility of requirements.

    The more uncertain you are of what you are doing, the less you will want to go down a path without verifying it (i.e. the shorter you will want your iterations to be).

4. The skills of your people.

   More emphasis will be placed on design reviews and code cleanup during the assessment period, so you will want to reach the assessments more quickly and frequently while your people are still learning how to develop high quality O-O designs.

2.1.4 The Number of Prerelease "Drivers"

Prerelease software drivers will usually coincide with major iterations, so that the number and timing of drivers match the number and timing of major iterations.[4] It is possible, of course, to schedule fewer "official" drivers. It is not likely that drivers can be scheduled at times other than major iteration assessment periods, since this is when functionality is complete.

Having multiple drivers scheduled gives the development group a chance to maintain interest and funding for the project. It also supports a solid base for efforts such as usability testing.

2.1.5 The Driver Functional Content

It is important to decide the basic functions to be implemented during a particular driver. This will be the high-level basis for the line item schedule for an iteration. Line items consist of *end user functions* to be delivered. *Functions*, as used here, are product capabilities that help solve end-user problems. They are **not** implementation algorithms in this context. Testing will focus on these end-user functions. The end user functions will be implemented via messaging to groups of objects that work together to provide these functions. The driver content (user functions) should be measured to monitor progress.

2.2 SUMMARY

The Iterative Development Process (IDP) is the framework for scheduling analysis and design activities. The goals of the IDP are:

1. To ensure the flexibility to build the *right* system by systematically verifying and refining requirements with customers at planned intervals.

2. To allow detailed plans to build complex systems that more closely match reality, by staging a rollout of the functions as more of the system is understood.

---

[4]*Drivers* as used here are not the same as software *builds*, which occur more frequently. Drivers are usable pieces of system functionality that are available at scheduled intervals in the overall product development effort. They are useful for user verification and usability testing.

The process is completed based on the satisfaction of the requirements.

A single iteration consists of a planning, production, and assessment period. The planning period starts an iteration by adapting to changing requirements, resources, schedules, and prerelease "driver" code contents. The production period is when the analysis, design, and implementation of the iteration line items occur. The assessment period completes the iteration. It is used to evaluate the system according to a variety of criteria, such as performance and reusability.

There will typically be three to six iterations, each of around 3 ½ months long, for a system of moderate size and complexity. Early release drivers that result from one or more of the iterations can be used for efforts such as usability testing.

Chapter 3

O-O Development Methodology

"The creation of a thousand forests is in one acorn."

Ralph Waldo Emerson

A software methodology provides a systematic set of steps to follow to help ensure that the *right* system is built and that it is *built right.* If the job is done well, you will end up with little "acorns" (business classes) that can be used to grow many "trees" (applications). It is worth noting that the methodology is object oriented, but an application developed using the O-O methodology can be object oriented or not.

This chapter discusses the methodology in general terms. Subsequent chapters address areas such as assessment emphasis and optional deliverables of different phases of development.

Figure 3.1 shows the types of development objects involved in the life cycle of O-O software.

The types of objects shown in the diagram indicate the key model objects that are created as part of the software development process.[1]

---

[1]There are UI classes that are a part of the application too, such as for windows. They are certainly an important part of the application, but are not focused on here. The requirements drive the definition of the model classes and the model classes drive

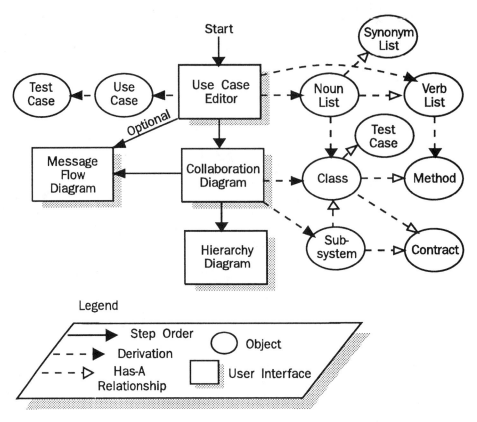

Figure 3.1   Object-Oriented Development Methodology

Not all of these types of methodology objects are required to be created during development and there is more than one way to create the
objects. For example, a *noun list* does not have to be created at all. It is
suggested that noun lists are useful when you are identifying the correct set of classes in the application, but the application can be created
without creating a noun list. If the noun list *is* created, it can be derived from the use cases (mini-scenarios for the system) or, alterna-
tively, the classes can be drawn directly on collaboration diagrams. In
both cases, you will look at similar information, such as nouns in the

---

the form and content of the UI classes. Different UI classes can be used with the same
underlying model classes to develop multiple applications. The separation of the UI
from the model is important for reusability.

system requirements or conversations with customers, to decide what items to include in the system being developed.

The *Has-A* relationship shown in the diagram is used to indicate which types of objects make up a class's state data. So, a *subsystem* has *classes* and *contracts*.

The ordering of the methodology steps are not lock-step activities. The *Use Case Editor* can be returned to after having worked on a *Collaboration Diagram*, for example. The idea of showing the order is to indicate the general sequence of activities. It makes sense to work on use cases before working on collaborations, which should be looked at before worrying about the inheritance hierarchy. Again, it is natural to bounce back and forth between some activities while developing the system. This is particularly evident when creating collaboration diagrams, which focus on classes, responsibilities, attributes, and collaborations. Bouncing between these is natural and should be encouraged. The attempt here is to set a general framework.

3.1 INPUTS

The inputs to the development effort come from:

1. **An initial requirements document (if it exists)**
   The business phase has an initial requirements document as a deliverable. This document was generated as part of the initial work on the product development, in determining the business case.
2. **Customer interviews**
   A key input for the effective development of any system is customer involvement. This is the primary technique for developing use cases, which are a useful (but not absolutely required) means of documenting the requirements and identifying the classes in the system.[2]
   As has been mentioned previously (but is worth reiterating), development depends upon customer involvement in the development effort.
3. **Existing system change requests**
   A good source of requirements for future efforts is, of course, any current customers using an existing predecessor or earlier version of the product.

---

[2]The term *use case* is from Ivar Jacobson, *The Industrial Development of Software Using an Object-Oriented Technique*, 1989.

4. Competitive products

   Changes in products in the marketplace are certainly inputs to future product development. These competitive pressures "raise the bar" of customer expectations and demands for functionality and usability.

5. Information from other tools

   For example, entity/relationship (E/R) information collected about the business entities in a CASE tool, such as Knowledge Ware's Information Engineering Workbench (IEW), can be used as inputs to begin the O-O analysis.

3.2 METHODOLOGY STEPS

The steps detailed in the following sections are not rigid steps, as in the waterfall methodology, but are fluid. During development, identification of classes, methods, and collaboration usually happens concurrently, as the design is explored. Often, abstract classes are discovered later and give some indication of hierarchical relationships for inheritance. In the absence of this abstraction, most classes are subclassed off of the inheritance tree root class (*Object* in Smalltalk) or declared as a base class (C++).

The emphasis is to examine the types of objects that exist in the problem domain. For example, Figure 3.2 shows class, relationship, and contract information for a subsystem in the sample ATM application.

These classes, the behaviors required from them as services, and how they work together are the result of an analysis of the requirements for the application. Looking at the list of requirements (page 2), we see mention of accounts (and types of accounts), types of transactions, and business policies. These are good indicators of classes needed to build an application to meet these requirements. Similarly, we see mention of requirements dealing with withdrawing and depositing funds. These may be the responsibilities of the *Account* class, resulting in available services, or behaviors. Relationships between classes, such as banks knowing about their customers, indicate how the classes can work together (collaboration). So, a bank may be able to ask a customer about his or her accounts.

Some classes may have common information and services. They can share this information by creating a common abstract superclass. For example, by having an abstract *Account* class, as well as *Savings-Account* and *CheckingAccount* classes, these classes can share services

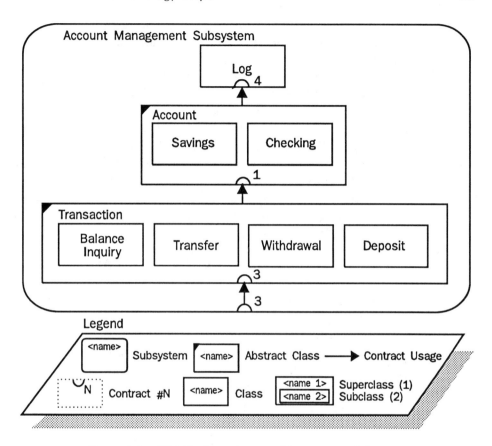

Figure 3.2   ATM Design—Account Management Subsystem

already defined, changing only what is necessary to provide their services properly.

As with any software development, it is necessary to understand the users' problem domain; in this example ATM machines and how they are used at banks. The process and methodology will help you to analyze the problem domain and create an application to meet the requirements, but it is still up to the developer to create a good design, in this case an O-O design.

3.2.1 Write Use Cases

As I said, use cases are mini-scenarios for the system. The idea is to focus on one usage of the system at a time. The use case is a *description* of the usage scenario, in terms the end user can understand. The intended users of the system have already been identified (before the development process began in the business phase: See Section 4.1, "Business Phase." The use cases are based on the tasks performed by the system users. Stick to fairly major tasks—don't write a use case for every action the user can take. For example, there should not be a "card entry" use case for the ATM application. The customers will certainly enter their cards when using the system, but this is merely a step toward the real functions being provided. Use cases are important in that they provide basic groundwork for the requirements document, user manual, and test cases.

The following use cases were identified from the initial requirements list for the ATM application:

ATM APPLICATION USE CASES

1. Balance inquiry
2. Account fund transfer
3. Cash withdrawal
   a. $200 maximum withdrawal per day (variation)
   b. default and specified withdrawal amount (variation)
4. Cash deposit
5. ATM access failure

The balance inquiry use case will be used for the examples that follow. The other use cases can be found in the complete ATM application documentation in Appendix D, "Complete ATM Application."

CURRENT SYSTEM
BALANCE INQUIRY

(Analyst) How do you currently handle account balance requests?

(A Teller) The way it works now is that the client writes their account number on a standard account form and gives the form plus some type of ID with their picture on it to the teller. The teller then makes sure it's the right person by entering the account number on the account query screen on their terminal and comparing the name on the ID to the name that comes up on the screen. Assuming it is the owner of the account, the teller then writes the balance and date on the account form and gives it to the client.

(Analyst)   What happens if it's not the account owner?

(A Teller)   That doesn't happen very often, but when it does, the teller verifies the account number with the client. If it still doesn't match, then the manager is called over to handle the problem.

(Analyst)   How do you get a balance for one of your accounts at the bank?

(A Bank Customer)   I usually just ask a teller to give me the balance for my account. They then ask me my account number and name, enter something on their computer, and tell me my balance. Sometimes they write it down for me too.

The current system information can then be used to identify classes in the system (such as *Account* and *Teller*), as well as their attributes (such as an account's *number* and *balance*) and responsibilities (such as reporting an account's current *balance*).

Understanding the system needs is valuable input to the design of the new system. The next step is to talk to the customer to understand the desired functionality for the new system.

DESIRED FUNCTIONS
BALANCE INQUIRY

(Analyst)   What capabilities would a system that handled account balance inquiries in the best possible way have?

(A Bank Customer)   I really don't want to have to wait for a teller to just get my account balance. I'd like to have access to the bank's information on me, such as through the terminals the tellers use. It would have to give me a slip with the amount on it, since I don't always have a pen and paper handy. And it wouldn't take too long to use—not too many steps. Oh, and I really don't want to have to remember my account number, if that would be possible—maybe I could just give my name. Of course, I wouldn't want other people to look at my information, so I guess there'd have to be some way to stop them.

(A Teller)   It really makes it difficult on us to keep up with the more important transactions during the day when we have to get people's balances for them. We certainly need a way to get to the balances for other reasons, but I don't want to have anything to do with an ordinary balance inquiry.

At this point, a use case for the new system function would be written and discussed with the customers, to make sure it meets their needs.

ATM USE CASE—BALANCE INQUIRY (ANALYSIS PHASE)

A terminal with a printer is made available to the customers in the lobby of the bank. It asks for the account number of the customer and then allows the customer to choose a function from a menu. If a balance inquiry is requested, the system prints a slip with the date, account name and number, and the balance amount.

Design information is included in the use case in order to make it easier to discuss with the customer, but this information is not part of the requirements. The goal is to extract the real underlying requirements.

Once the analyst discusses the use case with the customer, and makes any necessary changes, the use case is ready to be used for the analysis prototype. Once prototyped, the customer is again involved to verify that his or her needs are being met. Once the use case and prototype are verified, the analyst then extracts the requirements that have surfaced.

ATM BALANCE INQUIRY REQUIREMENTS

1. 24-hour access to balance information
2. Hard copy of balance amount
3. Security of information from invalid access

The focus during the analysis phase is on *what* is needed, and not *how* the needs are met. The use case would be updated during the design, so that it matches the evolving requirements and implementation. This updating may be done as part of the test group's responsibilities, since the use cases will largely make up the high-level test cases. The use cases will also provide a key input to the group responsible for producing a user's manual, since they document the major system functions.

Note: Tools that automate this portion of the effort should maintain the relationship between the use cases, the underlying requirements, and the implementation objects (classes, contracts, and so on).

ATM USE CASE—BALANCE INQUIRY (DESIGN PHASE)

A machine is available outside the bank for customers to perform typical teller functions. Customers have cards that have a unique identification and password that they insert into a slot in a card reader. The customer is prompted for the password that is inscribed on the card. If the two match, the customer is given a menu choice of actions on the screen. If the balance inquiry button is pressed, the customer is asked which account to use and a slip is printed which contains the account name and number, date, and amount of money in the account. The customer is allowed to then request another action, or to exit.

A single use case will typically relate to a group of line items in the development schedule. Relating this group of items and the use case will help in managing the development and test dependencies. This level of end-user function will typically be grouped together for parallel development in the project's major iterations.

3.2.2 Develop Message Flow Diagrams for Use Cases (Optional)

Message flow diagrams can be used for more than one purpose, including use case, method, and test case design. In this section, we focus on using them to document more detailed design information for a use case. Figure 3.3 shows a sample message flow diagram for the ATM application.

The message flow diagram shows a set of classes across the top and a time sequence from top to bottom. Shown within this table are message sends between classes, in the order they would occur according to the system design. This design documentation is useful to communicate what is being built. The message flows can be used for use case, test case, and method documentation. When used for method documentation, the message flow shows what messages would be sent by a single method to accomplish its task.

> **Note:** The messages shown should be the key *application-related* messages and not every message sent to accomplish the function. Focus on messages that are a part of contracts.

Figure 3.3 shows a *balanceInquiryFor:* message from the user (via the Interface subsystem) going to the *ATM* (with a *Customer* as a

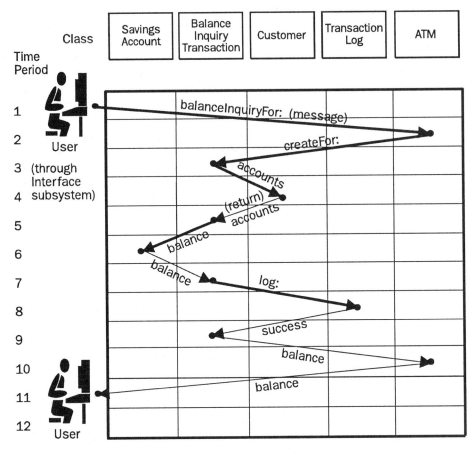

Figure 3.3 ATM Application Balance Inquiry Message Flow Diagram

parameter). The *ATM* then creates a *balanceInquiryTransaction* object, which then asks the *Customer* for his or her accounts.[3] The appropriate *savingsAccount* is then asked for its *balance*, which it returns. Next, the *BalanceInquiryTransaction* logs itself by a request to the *TransactionLog*. The *balance* is then returned to the *ATM*, from the original request. Finally, the original request result is returned to the user (again via the Interface subsystem).

---

[3]The *Customer* class as used here can be thought of as a *database* that holds information about the real person (the "user") that is the bank's customer. The *Customer* class provides that information on demand—in this case, it is the collection of *Account* objects that are associated with the person using the *ATM*.

3.2.3 Develop Collaboration Diagrams

Collaboration diagrams graphically depict classes, subsystems, contracts, and relationships between classes and subsystems. These diagrams are used during the analysis and design to document the system under development. The information on the diagrams can also be used to automate portions of the development process, such as the creation of class definition code as well as method selectors and comments. Figure 3.4 shows an example of a collaboration diagram. The

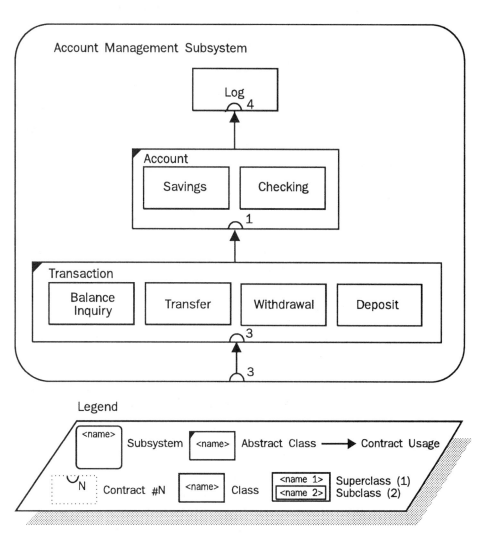

Figure 3.4 ATM Design–Account Management Subsystem Collaboration Diagram

following sections talk about how to gather the information to populate these diagrams.

The order of the activities in the following sections is flexible. Movement between activities to define the system is often rapid. The activities are also affected by the type of system being developed. For example, larger systems may define subsystems sooner in order to encapsulate "black-box" portions of the system, so that other areas can be concentrated on, possibly by different development teams.

There is a lot of potential information to show on the collaboration diagrams, and there are a number of ways to filter the information shown at any one time. Figure 3.5 shows *cardinality* for the relationships between the ATM application classes. Cardinality is an indication of the expected number of instances of each of the related object types. The use of cardinality is emphasized in Peter Coad's book on O-O analysis and is useful during design activities to determine class data implementation.

The *one-to-many* (1:M) has-a relationship indicates that the source class (the one the arrow points *away* from) holds a *collection* of the target class objects (the one the arrow points *toward*). For example, a single *Bank* has more than one *Customer,* so the *Bank* would have an instance variable that held a collection of customer objects. Similarly, a *one-to-one* (1:1) relationship would indicate that a single target class object is held by the source class, and so on.

A diagram view showing relationship cardinality in a more "Wirfs-Brock-like" manner is shown in Figure 3.6. Perhaps a tool that supports the Wirfs-Brock notation would also support this type of information view.

There are three main categories of relationships to map to an O-O system design:

1. is-a

   This type of relationship results in the source class becoming a subclass of the target class. For example, a *CdAccount is-a SavingsAccount.* This type of relationship is generally shown via the inheritance class hierarchy or as a nested class in the Wirfs-Brock notation.

2. has-a

   This type of relationship results in the source class containing (collaborating with) one or more instances of the target class, depending on the cardinality.

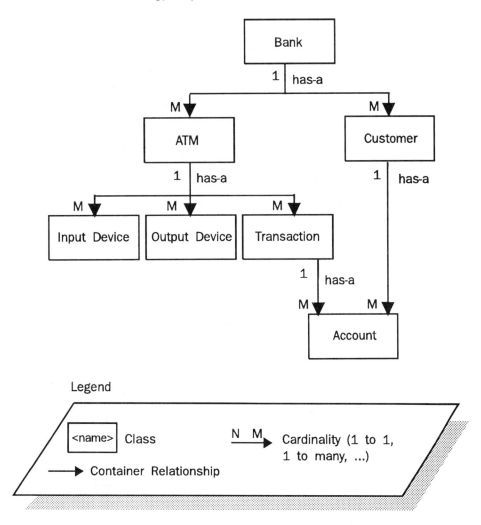

Figure 3.5   ATM Design–Cardinality Relationships

3. other

Any relationship that doesn't fit the previous two may result in a responsibility (method) requirement on the target class. For example, if a *writes to* relationship is shown between a *Transaction* (source) and *TransactionLog* (target), the *TransactionLog* class probably will have a *write:* method in the design. Some "other" relationships may be handled without an explicit method. For

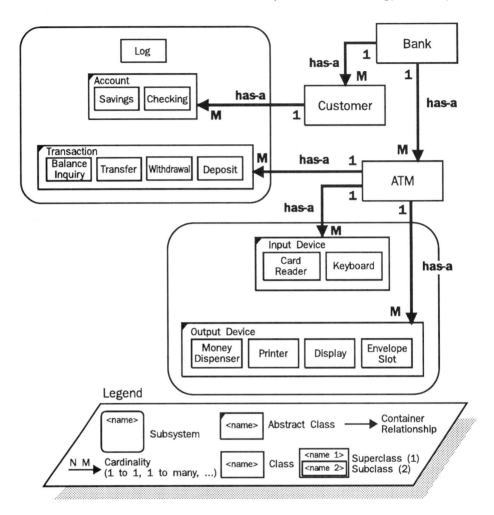

Figure 3.6 ATM Design–Cardinality Relationships Alternate View

example, if an *ATM* "creates" a *Transaction,* inheriting the object creation capability (*new* in Smalltalk) will handle this relationship requirement. This relationship would still be shown on the collaboration diagram.

Cardinality information is not required. Indicators such as plural forms of instance variable names, for example, can be used in place of a *has-a* relationship. Cardinality merely documents business and design information more blatantly—and some people are comfortable using E/R diagrams. Again, it is another way of viewing system information—if it helps you, use it. Just be aware that E/R diagramming is just a notation—it doesn't guarantee that the right objects will be shown on the diagram.

3.2.3.1 Identify classes

Lists of key nouns can be gathered from requirements documentation and/or use cases as potential classes. Since these documents discuss the problem domain being addressed by the application under development, the descriptions will likely talk, either directly or indirectly, about the types of objects in that domain. The names used should be in the *customers'* terms.

Try to extract the key nouns in the application domain. Be alert to synonyms, such as *clients* and *customers*. In selecting classes, look for:[4]

1. *Tangible things,* such as people or business forms.
2. *Systems outside the current application,* such as the payroll system.
3. *Devices the system interacts with,* such as a printer or telephone.
4. *Locations of things,* such as an ATM machine or account.
5. *Roles of people or systems,* such as client or teller.
6. *Organizations,* such as the bank or department.
7. *Events,* such as opening an account or changing a traffic light.
8. *Remembered events,* such as the time of a transaction or date an account was opened.

Include existing business classes as necessary. Do not include *base* classes, such as *Integer, Collection,* or *String.* These will only clutter the diagrams, adding no application-level meaning to the design view.

For example, remember the ATM requirements stated by the customer to the analyst:

ATM CUSTOMER
REQUIREMENTS DRAFT

1. 24-hour access to:
   a. savings and checking accounts
   b. Move money between accounts
   c. Withdraw cash
      1) Default amount
      2) Specified amount
   d. Deposit money to an account
   e. Get an account balance

[4]The list is derived from Grady Booch, *Object-Oriented Design with Applications* (Redwood City, CA: Benjamin/Cummings Publishing Co.,1990), p. 141.

2. Log transactions
3. Cancel a transaction at any time before it is submitted
4. Failure security
   a. Card kept if too many invalid attempts
5. Multiple transactions for a single access
6. Business policies
   $200/day withdrawal limit

The following nouns were taken from these requirements:

───────────────────── **ATM NOUN LIST** ─────────────────────

- savingsAccount
- checkingAccount
- money
- account
- transaction
- card
- business policy

Figure 3.7 shows the content for documenting the classes.[5]

The *private* responsibilities are those used by this class to do its work and should *not* be used by other classes. The *contracts* group public services that are available to other classes and/or subsystems.

IDENTIFY CLASS ATTRIBUTES: The information that a class remembers to maintain its state is called an *attribute*. For example, an account remembers its *balance* and a bank remembers its *accounts*. These are state data for these objects. During implementation, the attributes normally become instance variables.[6]

An alternative to keeping information in an attribute is to collaborate with another class via a message to get the information.

───────────

[5]This format is derived from Rebecca Wirfs-Brock et al., *Designing Object-Oriented Software* (Englewood Cliffs, NJ: Prentice Hall, 1990), p. 138.

[6]State data can be kept in more global locations, such as class variables or system global storage. This is less desirable, but is sometimes needed. For example, a global area in Smalltalk is sometimes used to hold the "system" object that represents the "top-level" object in the system. This object is used to get the ball rolling. For example, the *Bank* object for our ATM application might be kept in a global variable to make it accessible to a variety of applications.

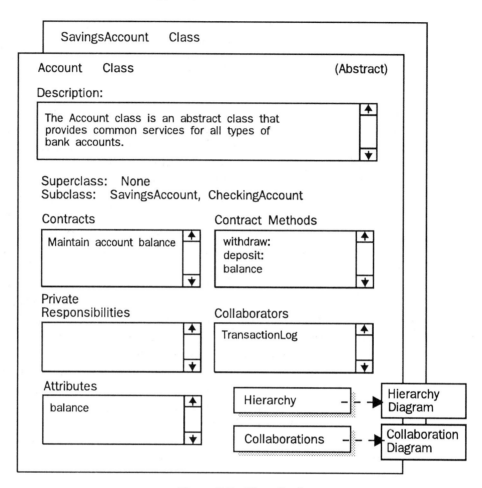

Figure 3.7 Class Cards

Simple information, such as strings to hold an account name, are usually kept as an attribute. Information that can be derived, such as the customer's total assets in the bank, can either be calculated when needed or kept in storage, depending on the system requirements (speed versus space). Be aware that *every* piece of state data is kept in *every* instance of a class. Keep the information where it logically belongs. This is hopefully where it is used the most.

Look over the class list, making an attribute instead of a class when that makes sense. This most frequently occurs when a class is really just providing the functions of a base system class, such as *String*. For example, if an *AccountNumber* class was postulated, it may be found to just provide the functions of an integer and should really be an attribute of the *Account* class.

3.2.3.2 Identify responsibilities (methods)

As the lists of nouns are gathered (see Section 3.2.3.1, "Identify Classes"), verbs or verb phrases can also be gathered. These verbs should be associated with the nouns that provide the actions in the description (there can be no action without an object to act upon).

State the responsibilities as generally as possible. Add specifics only when necessary. Specifics will limit the amount of reuse. Obviously, the responsibilities must fulfill their intent but can still be built with reuse in mind. For example, a *depositMoneyToChecking* method is less generic than a *depositMoney* method, even though both provide the same function. The latter is more desirable, since it can be reused by most of the account types in the bank.

The names for classes and methods are very important. In an O-O system, the development should result in a system that is implemented in the *problem-domain language*. By this, I mean that the terms used in the problem domain, such as a bank's use of ATM machines, make it into the code. So, logic should be almost readable by your end users, with statements like *currentAccount withdraw: anAmount*.

The responsibilities should have a correspondence with the attributes assigned to a class. The attributes will be used in the methods that fulfill the responsibilities.

For example, the following verbs are taken from the ATM initial requirements statement (page 43) for the indicated nouns already gathered:

──────── **ATM VERB LIST** ────────

NOUN	ASSOCIATED VERBS
savingsAccount	moveMoney
	withdrawCash
	depositMoney
	getBalance
checkingAccount	moveMoney
	withdrawCash
	depositMoney
	getBalance
money	(none)
account	moveMoney
	withdrawCash

	depositMoney
	getBalance
transaction	log
	cancel
card	keep
businessPolicy	limitWithdrawal

Not all classes take an active role in the application. *Money*, for example, at this point in time is a passive participant. It is certainly involved in account transactions, but at a high level does not itself drive the activities.

Also, some initial assignments may have to be reexamined. For instance, *keep* is probably a behavior for the *cardReader* class and not the *card* class. In order to make method names more readable, we'll drop "get" and "put" from the front of the verb phrases. So, "getBalance" becomes "balance," resulting in logic that reads like *myAccount balance*.

The overlap in function in the three account classes indicates the common services that can be pulled into a shared, abstract class. In this case, the *Account* class would be an abstract superclass of both *checkingAccount* and *savingsAccount*. This will create an application "mini-hierarchy," containing classes which are all contained within the application. The subclasses should support *all* the responsibilities of the superclass. If the subclass doesn't support them all, then look at a different location for the classes and responsibilities.

3.2.3.3 Identify subsystems

The subsystems are major portions of the system, broken at logical functional cohesion boundaries.[7] Look for strong coupling between classes to find candidates for subsystems. If groups of classes mostly deal with each other, they may be able to be contained in a subsystem. If you can give the group of classes a meaningful name, you probably have a good grouping. This grouping helps in human understanding of the system, especially for large systems. Even in a system of moderate size, the number of classes can be in the hundreds and the number of methods can be in the thousands! In the case of a large system,

---

[7]Subsystems are similar in intent to what Bertrand Meyer refers to as *clusters* in "The New Culture of Software Development: Reflections on the Practice of Object-Oriented Design," *Technology of Object Oriented Languages and Systems Proceedings (TOOLS)*, 1989, pp. 13–23.

subsystems may need to be identified earlier, to help manage the complexity. In this case, break the system along major functionality boundaries rather than class collaboration and cohesion boundaries (since you won't have classes yet).

For example, classes that have to do with account transaction processing at a bank may be grouped into an account management subsystem (see Figure 3.4). The subsystems facilitate hiding details of the system, depending on the level desired. So, the details of the account management subsystem may be hidden when the developer is focusing on the interface subsystem. The subsystems also provide the point for controlling architected interfaces, called *contracts*. Figure 3.8 shows the subsystems for the ATM application. A diagram such as this would be appropriate early in the development of a large system. A smaller system, manageable by a team of less than 15 people, could delay looking at subsystems until after they have a better understanding of the classes involved in the problem domain.

Figure 3.9 shows the content for documenting the subsystems.[8]

3.2.3.4 Identify contracts

Contracts are logical groupings of key, high-level responsibilities for a subsystem.[9] They are delegated to class(es) within the subsystem to service. The contracts are the architected interfaces to a part of the system. Contracts are especially important for large systems, providing points of control between the small teams of developers working on different parts of the same product, and for (future) reusable components in your reuse library, providing documented interfaces to facilitate black-box reuse.

If a subsystem has a large number of contracts, then too much of the system responsibility may have been given to the subsystem. It is possible that the classes need to be regrouped to reduce the number of classes and increase the cohesion within the group. Rethink the subsystem name in this case. Again, if no meaningful name is evident, then keep working at it. Only the services provided to subsystems and classes *outside* a particular subsystem should be assigned at the subsystem level (versus a class-to-class contract *within* a subsystem).

---

[8]This format is derived from Rebecca Wirfs-Brock et al., *Designing Object-Oriented Software* (Englewood Cliffs, NJ: Prentice Hall, 1990), p. 137.

[9]See Bertrand Meyer, *Object-oriented Software Construction* (Englewood Cliffs, NJ: Prentice Hall, 1988) for a look at the use of contracts in *Eiffel*. Meyer takes a different slant than Wirfs-Brock. He focuses on formalizing the contracts in the code to make sure that the state is as expected at the start and end of a method.

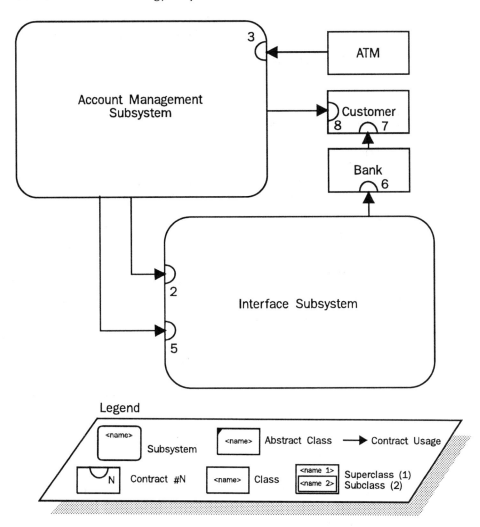

Figure 3.8   ATM Collaboration Diagram–ATM Application

The contracts identify how the classes and subsystems will work together (collaborate) to provide a function. They are a level of abstraction that hides details and lets you focus on the main intent of a class or subsystem. A subclass must support any contracts of its superclass(es). Also, for other classes or subsystems to claim support for a contract, they must provide logically equivalent methods for each of the contract's detailed responsibilities (of the same name). If you find a class that does not collaborate with other classes, you have either

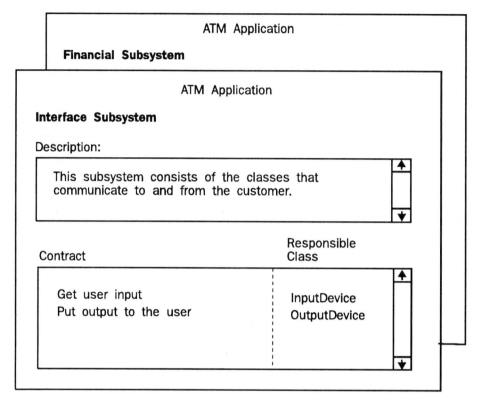

Figure 3.9 Subsystem Cards

missed part of the functionality of the system or the class is not needed in the application.

In looking at the ATM application, the account management subsystem may have the responsibility to *maintain account balances.* This may include services dealing with deposits and withdrawals. The contract will be mapped to a specific class and method that is responsible to service the request for the subsystem's clients. Contracts are identified by the services requested by clients *outside* the subsystem.

Figure 3.10 shows the content for documenting the contracts.[10]

Contracts are a key part of the controlled architecture of the system and should be relatively stable from release to release. They are

---

[10]This format is derived from Rebecca Wirfs-Brock et al., *Designing Object-Oriented Software* (Englewood Cliffs, NJ: Prentice Hall, 1990), p. 264.

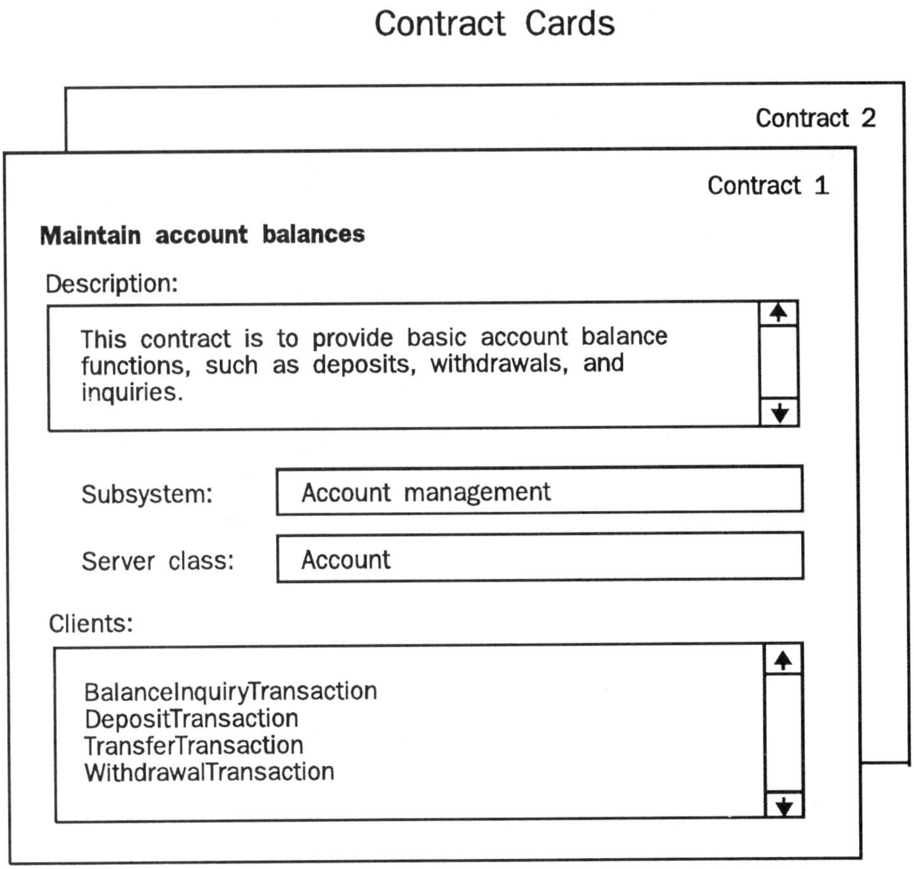

Contract Cards

Figure 3.10   Contract Cards

public services that are expected to be made available for the system to work as required. Changes to the underlying implementation of the contract are controlled by the build and quality processes, while the definition of the contracts themselves are controlled by the architecture document change process.

In looking for contracts, the developer looks for the types of services that the subsystem or class is expected to provide. The class responsibilities derived from use cases and requirements are the best place to look for functional groupings that end up becoming contracts. For example, methods such as *moveMoney*, *withdrawCash*, *depositMoney*, and *getBalance* are all related to account management.

Wirfs-Brock has suggested that you may want to reflect the expected message volume in different line thicknesses for the collaboration lines on the diagrams.[11] This is additional system design information and is worth considering.

3.2.4 Place Classes in the Inheritance Hierarchy

Once you are ready to focus on the implementation details for your application, you will want to decide where in the class hierarchy to locate your classes in order to optimize the reuse gains through inheritance.[12] Remember, you have already developed mini-hierarchies that specifically relate to your application (see Figure 3.11). Only the classes that have hierarchical relationships *within the ATM application itself* are shown in the diagram. They certainly inherit from classes outside the application classes as well, but this is an implementation detail and not an application design issue.

These mini-hierarchies allow a single-mindedness of responsibility. For example, the different types of transaction classes do not have to have type-checking code such as *IF* statements in them, since they only do one type of action. The abstract class, *Transaction*, allows all types of transactions to understand common functions, such as logging themselves, again simplifying the code. The subclasses are coded according to their unique differences, such as a *Withdrawal Transaction* checking to ensure a positive balance (if that's the bank's policy).

Abstractions sometimes have limited value. The *OutputDevice* abstract class certainly provides organization to the class hierarchy that helps people understand the system better, but since the types of output devices are so different, there is little commonality of code. It is questionable whether this abstract class should be created or not; I will leave it as a point of debate for the reader.

The location of the classes in the hierarchy will depend on the answers to a number of questions:

1. Is the class part of the user interface?

    If so, it may need to be subclassed within an application window framework. For example, you may have a *BaseWindow* class with a *TextualWindow* subclass in the system that gives you basic

---

[11]Rebecca Wirfs-Brock et al., *Designing Object-Oriented Software* (Englewood Cliffs, NJ: Prentice-Hall, 1990), p. 139.

[12]See Mark Lorenz, "Real World Reuse," *Journal of Object-Oriented Programming (JOOP)*, (November/December 1991), pp. 35–39 for more information about application versus class hierarchy focus, a detailed look at the hierarchy, and help in positioning classes in the hierarchy.

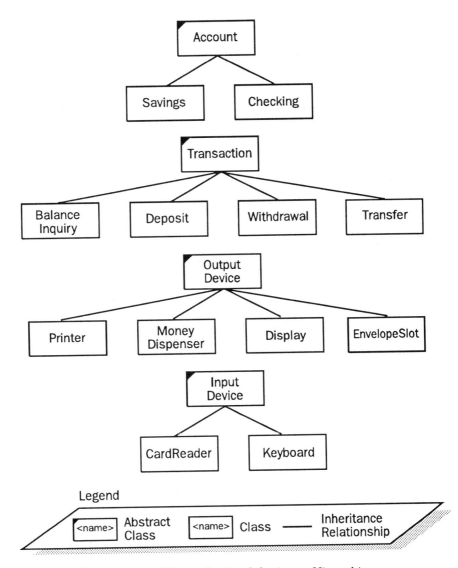

Figure 3.11 ATM Application Inheritance Hierarchies

window and text entry services. To implement a *CustomerRecord Window* class, you would subclass *TextualWindow* (and thereby *BaseWindow*).

It may be desirable when designing reusable frameworks to show them on their own subsystem collaboration diagram, with intended subclassing locations shown via an empty class box drawn with dotted lines.

2. Do the class instances persist?

If so, the class may need to be subclassed within a persistent object framework. Object database management systems (ODBMS) may have a persistent framework or they may allow instances to send a message to transform themselves into persistent objects, no matter where their class is located in the hierarchy. Persistence means that the ODBMS will manage the object's storage and class membership for you.

3. Does the class have similar behaviors to another class in the system?

If so, the class may be a specialization of that class and would work well as a subclass. For example, if at a later time a *CdAccount* class was added to the hierarchy, it would share many attributes and services with *Account* and *SavingsAccount*, as well as being of a logically similar type of object. It would become a subclass of *SavingsAccount*.

You want to try to avoid subclassing by *convenience*. It is convenient to subclass a class that will give you some methods and/or instance variables that you could use, even if the new subclass is not of the same type (or plays the same role) as the superclass. This will cause future maintenance problems, since the changes to one of the classes will probably not be desired by (and may be disastrous for!) the other class. You should think about whether the new subclass can be used in any context as the superclass.[13]

Frederic Wild advocates that subclasses either inherit *all* the superclass's methods, only adding new methods and instance variables that work with the superclass's structure, or the new class should be positioned elsewhere.[14] These are good indicators to look for to judge whether a potential position is good or not.

If there is some part of a class that you can reuse, but the class is not a similar type of object, you are better off copying the desired code and working from there in another location in

---

[13]M. Sakkinen discusses this further in "Disciplined Inheritance," *Proceedings of the 1989 European Conference on Object-Oriented Programming (ECOOP)*, pp. 39–56.

[14]Frederic H. Wild III, "Managing Class Coupling," *Unix Review*, 9, No. 10 (October 1991), pp. 45–47.

the hierarchy. The desired code will probably change anyway, since the code will probably need to be tailored to the new object type.

3.2.5 Develop Message Flow Diagrams for Methods (optional)

Message flow diagrams are useful for designing and documenting the logic in a method. The flows show what messages are sent to which application classes to accomplish the desired function. Since methods should be short (three to six lines of code), the message flow diagrams should also be short. Only show messages that are important to the application (i.e., don't bother drawing flows for minute implementation details, such as a message to convert a string to a symbol). Also, you may not bother with a flow diagram for simple methods, such as accessing methods.

3.2.6 Implement Methods

You want to focus on the public protocols (contracts) for the class. Private "support" methods will come about naturally as you go.

Code the methods in either the prototype language, for the analysis phase, or the product target language, for the design and test phase. These may be the same or different languages. The language used should support O-O constructs (class, inheritance, polymorphism). If you implement an application that has an O-O design in a non-O-O language, you will have to "manually" work around the language restrictions—no simple task. Given the plethora of O-O languages (Smalltalk, C++ Objective-C, Eiffel, Object Pascal, and so on), you should be able to find one that meets your requirements. Other languages will follow, I'm sure (COBOL++??).

Coding standards my projects have used for Smalltalk are in Appendix J.3, "Smalltalk Coding Standards." Standards for C++ are in Appendix J.4, "C++ Coding Standards." Be sure to read Appendix J.2, "Common Coding Standards," for both languages. You will have to develop your own standards for other languages, such as Objective-C or Eiffel, but the guidelines listed should be helpful in that effort.

Wild advises that coupling lessons from structured techniques have applicability for class designs.[15] He advocates the use of *interface*

---

[15]Ibid.

coupling, which does not allow one class to access another class's data, even if it is a subclass. He advises against *internal* coupling, where the data of another class are manipulated directly. The reasoning is that maintenance is more difficult for tightly coupled classes. I would generally agree. I think if you do a good job of positioning a class in the hierarchy, you won't have much trouble with coupling. There are also cases, such as abstract classes, where you are *intended* to manipulate another class's data when you are a subclass. These are concerns to keep in mind as you develop your method logic.

Debugging can be complicated by the inheritance hierarchy. If a subclass invokes a superclass's functionality in addition to the overriding method's logic, there can be side effects from the modified actions upon receipt of the message. Again, if you can keep the internal coupling to a minimum, you will have fewer problems. Purchase discusses different types of bugs found in O-O systems, along with their implications for debug support.[16]

Another issue is: "How do you debug *abstract classes?*" The answer is that you can't, directly. You will have to exercise the abstract class code via the subclass(es).

3.2.6.1 Test methods

Developers are responsible to unit test their own classes. The focus should be on *public* methods. In exercising public methods, all private methods should be used. Delete any private methods not used, directly or indirectly, to support public methods. Exceptions to this rule are the "support" methods, such as *classComment* and *example* (see Apperdix J.3, "Smalltalk Coding Standards").

It may be desirable to develop test cases *before* developing the class to be tested. This may help the developers focus on what is to be accomplished, without cluttering their minds with how they solved the problems. See Section 4.3.2, "Test Overview," for a discussion of O-O test and a testing strategy.

3.2.7 Develop Function Tests

The use cases delivered early in the development effort are good inputs as a starting point for *function* test cases. As build code is delivered on a weekly basis, the test team should be finalizing and running function tests on completed pieces. The test cases will iterate along with the system under development and will be the primary inputs,

---

[16]Jan A. Purchase and Russel L. Winder, "Debugging tools for object-oriented programming," *Journal of Object-Oriented Programming* (June 1991), pp. 10–27.

in their final form, for the system test at the end of the design and test phase.

An input for a function test is the status from development of the function schedules, so that the test team can coordinate their efforts with those of the development team. A deliverable of a function test is a list of *intra*departmental problem reports. These reports are handled quickly by the development team for the next build(s).

*Inter*departmental problem reports are written during *system* test, formally documenting the results of the system "selloff" (certification that it meets all requirements).

3.3 SUMMARY

A software methodology provides a systematic set of steps to follow to help ensure that the *right* system is built and that it is *built right*. The emphasis is to examine the types of objects that exist in the problem domain.

The ordering of the methodology steps are not lock-step activities, but rather a general sequence of activities. It is natural to bounce back and forth between some activities while developing the system. This is particularly evident when creating collaboration diagrams, which focus on classes, responsibilities, attributes, and collaborations. Bouncing between these is natural and should be encouraged.

3.3.1 Methodology Steps

1. Write use cases.

    Use cases are mini-scenarios for the system. The idea is to focus on one usage of the system at a time. The goal is to extract the real underlying requirements.

2. Develop message flow diagrams for use cases (optional).

    Message flow diagrams show key application-related message sends between classes, in the order they would occur according to the system design.

3. Develop collaboration diagrams.

    Collaboration diagrams graphically depict classes and subsystems, along with indications of other classes and subsystems they collaborate with.

    a. Identify classes.

        Lists of key nouns can be gathered from requirements documentation and/or use cases as potential classes. Try to extract the key nouns in the application domain.

b. Identify class attributes.

The information that a class remembers to maintain its state is called an *attribute*.

c. Identify responsibilities (methods).

As the lists of nouns are gathered, verbs or verb phrases can also be gathered. These verbs should be associated with their related nouns.

d. Identify subsystems.

The subsystems are major portions of the system, broken at logical functional cohesion boundaries. Look for strong coupling between classes to find candidates.

e. Identify contracts.

Contracts are key, high-level responsibilities for a class or subsystem.

4. Place classes in the inheritance hierarchy.

Once you are ready to focus on the implementation details for your application, you will want to decide where in the class hierarchy to locate your classes in order to optimize the reuse gains through inheritance.

5. Develop message flow diagrams for methods (optional).

Message flow diagrams are useful for designing and documenting the logic in a method.

6. Implement methods.

You want to focus on the public protocols (contracts) for the class first. Private "support" methods will come about naturally as you go.

7. Test methods.

The developers are responsible to unit test their own classes. The focus should be on *public* methods.

8. Develop function tests.

The use cases delivered early in the development effort are good inputs as a starting point for function test cases. As build code is delivered on a weekly basis, the test team should be finalizing and running function tests on completed pieces. The test cases will iterate along with the system.

Chapter 4

Software Development Phases

*"The doctor can bury his mistakes but an architect
can only advise his clients to plant vines."*

Frank Lloyd Wright

In developing software, we are trying to build what the customer wants in the most profitable manner possible. This means we build the best product on the market in the lowest-cost manner. In order to do this, a four-phase approach is recommended:

PHASES

1. Business
2. Analysis
3. Design and Test
4. Packaging

These are each briefly discussed in this overview section, with a detailed discussion in the related sections that follow. The relationships between the phases are shown in Figure 4.1.

There are a few points worth noting right at the start.

Development Phases

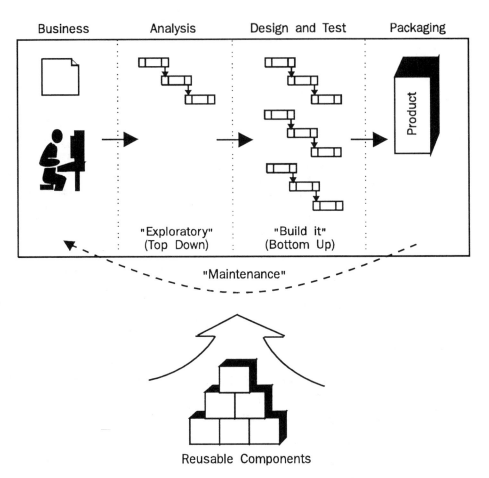

Figure 4.1 Software Development Process Overview

1. The analysis and design and test phases contain aspects of the life cycle that are typically shown separately, such as implementation. This is due to the fact that prototyping and iterative development are going on during these phases. The traditional phases aren't shown because they are not separate time periods in the development process where the emphasis is on them, such as in the waterfall approach.

2. "Maintenance" is not included in the phases. This is not to say that existing software is not addressed in this book. On the contrary, it is worth explicitly stating that *maintenance is the same as*

development. New O-O code being developed can be interfaced to existing system(s). Interface classes can be used to transition between the new O-O system and the old system. Obviously, if the existing system is object oriented, then the job will be easier. But if it is not object oriented, there are many ways to communicate with it, such as Dynamic Data Exchange (DDE) and Dynamic Link Libraries (DLLs).

3. By having the design and test phase follow the analysis phase, the focus starts with the *problem domain* and *then* the *solution domain.* In other words, the developer works with classes and abstractions that relate to the users' world first and only afterward worries about where to put the classes in the hierarchy. I view the activities in an O-O development as "meet in the middle"—the analysis activities focus on top-down discovery of new business objects; the design activities focus on bottom-up reuse through inheritance and delegation.

    There is certainly a lot carried over between the analysis and design phases, including clear requirements, key class definitions, and a running prototype. The division between the two is not a hard line. The phases are divided to emphasize the difference in focus and goals between exploring the requirements using prototype code (analysis) and building the system using production code (design). I have seen time and again that the first iteration(s) on something should be thrown away. Certainly, carry the key classes and their public protocols across to design, but don't assume that the prototype *as is* will make the transition. Ship a product, not a prototype.

4. The *same* (small) team is developing the application across both the analysis and design phases. There may certainly be personnel changes during the development (expect an impact!) and people may change "hats" (analyst, application developer, tester, class programmer, and so on), but the intent is that there is no disconnect as deliverables are "thrown over the wall." See Appendix F, "Development Team Roles," for a discussion of the different roles people play.

5. One final topic that deserves special attention—separation of the application model from the UI. The development of the model of the application classes and the UI to access the model is depicted in Figure 4.2.

The model and UI are shown as separate, parallel paths because it is important to keep the two relatively independent. The main reason for

Business	Analysis	Design and Test	Packaging

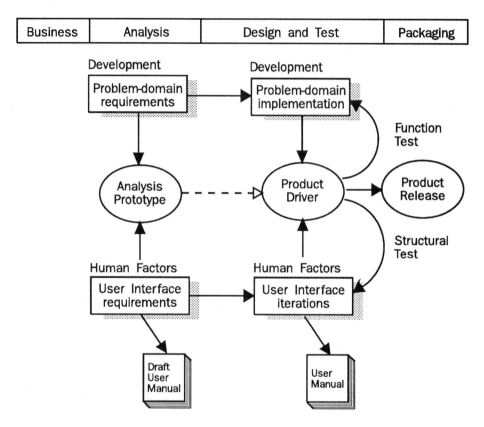

Figure 4.2   Model and UI Development Overview

this is that the model for your business can be reused in many different ways with very little change. For example, you could decide to use a mouse to select ATM options on a screen for an ATM application. You could then change the application to use a card reader and function buttons on totally different hardware and *the underlying function would be largely unaffected.* You could also develop a new application using many of the same classes and methods of the model of your business by driving them via different UI objects (see Figure 4.3). In fact, you can certainly have a batch application that has little or no UI.

Developing a good UI is an important and difficult task, but it is a *completely different* task from developing the model of the associated application. It is suggested that the usability group take the lead in flushing out the requirements for the UI and designing it, with development providing the implementation support when the time is right.

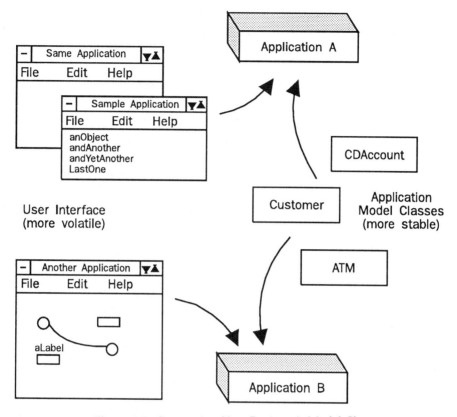

Figure 4.3 Leveraging Your Business's Model Classes

See Sankar for a further discussion of the activities the usability people should provide on a project.[1]

Resist putting UI details as requirements (this would cause unnecessary ripples in the requirements document). Stick to the underlying requirements for the UI. Examples of valid UI requirements:

- Fields x and y need to appear together and field z should be accessible from there.
- Standard form 32-A needs to be presented to the user as it would be printed.
- The item price should be displayed after its product code is scanned at the register.
- A mouse cannot be required to access the system's functions.

[1]Chetan S. Sankar and Walter H. Hawkins, "The Role of User Interface Professionals in Large Software Projects," *IEEE Transactions on Professional Communication*, 34, No. 2, (June 1991), pp. 94–99.

- The Common User Access (CUA) standards set in the 1991 document will be followed.

These are probably not UI requirements:

- A mouse will be used to highlight text by holding button 1 down while dragging the cursor over the text. (What happens if the way highlighting is done changes? Is the real requirement that a mouse can be used for highlighting? Or something else?)
- The Options pulldown will have an item called "Set search space . . . " on it. (What if the text changes? Is the real requirement that the search space be tailorable? If so, then this is a model class requirement, which is surfaced *in some way* to the user.)

As with any requirements, they should focus on the *what* part of the user functional requirements. The *how* should be left to the object-oriented analysis, design, and implementation.

The overall goal of the development phases is to set up a structure for building and delivering a quality product that meets the customer's needs. The following sections discuss each phase, focusing on the key software development phases: **analysis** and **design and test.**

4.1 BUSINESS PHASE

The business phase starts the software development process going. This phase's activities are done once (versus iteratively) before the start of the analysis phase. The focus of this section is on the initial business activities that directly affect the software development effort described here. There will certainly be specific business activities that your company may do that are not listed here. You may need to look at any possible implications of these additional activities, requirements, and/or deliverables your company has.

4.1.1 Prerequisites

The business phase has the following prerequisites:

1. User demand for a new system.
2. Customer willingness to participate in a system development effort.

4.1.2 Activities

The business phase has the following activities:

1. Identify and document types of users.

2. Identify and document initial user requirements.

3. Contact customers interested in a development partnership.

4.1.2.1 Identify and document types of users

It is important to be clear about who the system is for. For example, is the system for professional programmers (i.e., scientific programmers, systems programmers, business programmers), business professionals (i.e., coders of spreadsheet cells, users of many complex tools, casual users), or computer novices?

The decision about what type of person the system is for will have profound impacts on design decisions. It is difficult to build a system that does not require much training. It is even more difficult to build a system that does not require much training and is flexible. Make sure you know who you're building the system for, so you can make the optimum decisions along the way.

4.1.2.2 Contact customers interested in a development partnership

Once you know the type of user you are targeting, you can start looking for potential customers that are willing to work together for the product development. The benefits to emphasize for the customers are:

1. Early driver usage

2. Discounted product purchase price

3. Direct input to product content

This step is absolutely critical to the success of the remaining efforts. Validation of requirements and usability testing will not be possible without customer involvement.

4.1.2.3 Identify and document initial customer requirements

The reason for starting the system development came from somewhere: discussions with customers at users' conferences, changes in the competition in the marketplace, or internal research efforts. Whatever the impetus, take those ideas with you to meet with the customers.

The initial discussions with the customers involved in the development should be documented in notes and/or use cases that will be used as inputs for the requirements document. Appendix E, "Requirements Specification Outline," details an outline for a requirements document. As much as possible, the requirements document should be just that: *requirements and not design*. The discussions should focus on end-user functionality necessary to be productive at the tasks at hand.

During the initial business phase, the goal is to put together high-level requirements and not an entire document. That is the major output of the analysis phase. The draft of the requirements document should be a framework for the work ahead.

4.1.3 Deliverables

The business phase has the following deliverables:

1. Initial customer requirements document draft.

   This document will contain the initial system requirements.

2. Statement of target customer.

   This includes a statement of the type of customer as well as a list of customers willing to participate in the development effort.

4.1.4 ATM Application Initial Requirements

The initial requirements are repeated here to make it easier to follow the activities described in the development phases.

ATM CUSTOMER REQUIREMENTS DRAFT

The initial requirements stated by the users of the system to the system analysts are:

1. 24-hour access to:
   a. Access savings and checking accounts
   b. Move money between accounts
   c. Withdraw cash
      1) Default amount
      2) Specified amount
   d. Deposit money to an account
   e. Get an account balance
2. Log transactions
3. Cancel a transaction at any time before it is submitted
4. Failure security
   a. Card kept if too many invalid attempts
5. Multiple transactions for a single access
6. Business policies
   a. $200/day withdrawal limit

4.2 ANALYSIS PHASE

The analysis phase uses an iterative prototyping technique to develop its deliverables. Even though it is called the analysis phase, it has design and implementation characteristics of an iterative development. The emphasis, however, is on the system analysis and corresponding documentation of a detailed requirements specification and system architecture draft. This focus is more of a "top-down" identification of new reusable business components. The feasibility of the project can also be verified during this activity. Iterative development is the most effective means to these ends.

An assumption is that the analysis iterations produce a *prototype*, which will not be directly used to develop the final product (the design and test phase iterations do evolve into the final product). The reason to insist that the prototype is thrown away is that the emphasis during analysis is *not* on code quality, reuse, or performance. The emphasis is on flushing out requirements (problem space). The code is "quick and dirty." During design, the emphasis switches to high quality code (solution space).

The IDP iterations will tend to be shorter in the analysis phase than during the design and test phase. One- to two-month iterations will not be atypical, with a very short planning period and medium length production and assessment periods. The analyst must be careful to make sure that the efforts stay focused on documenting requirements and not on building the product. The volume of pure requirements will remain manageable if design does not creep in. Design is also much more volatile than requirements.

Scheduling will be largely driven by discussions and evaluations with the customer. The work is exploratory, geared toward flushing out requirements details. The areas to work on during an iteration should be the least understood, highest-risk areas. Once the requirements for an area are firm, that area should not be worked on again, *no matter what the state of the prototype code for that area* (remember—the prototype is *throwaway!*).

The emphasis during the IDP production period is on developing enough functionality to allow effective customer involvement during the assessment period. The emphasis during the IDP assessment period is on customer involvement. It is key that representatives of the targeted customer set be involved in verifying the requirements, since they are *their* requirements, not the analysts' requirements!

Figure 4.4 shows the analysis phase prerequisites and deliverables, which are discussed in the following sections.

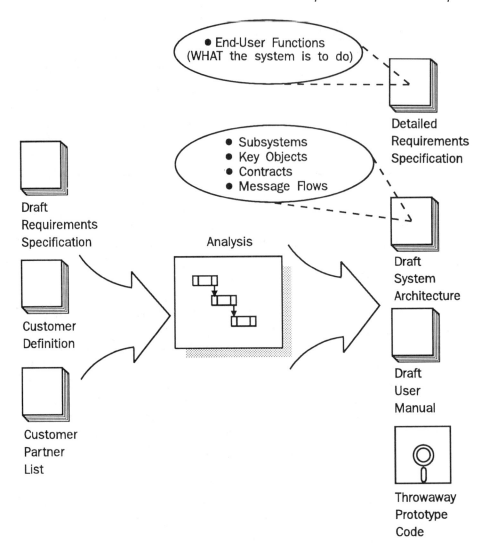

Figure 4.4   Analysis-Phase Prerequisites and Deliverables

4.2.1 Prerequisites

Before the analysis phase can begin, certain deliverables of the business phase must be completed:

1. Requirements specification draft
   This is a starting set of requirements, gathered up front by planners and/or analysts working with customers to determine new requirements.

2. Customer definition

   This is a statement of the intended type of user of the system. For example, the user may be a business professional, comfortable with coding spreadsheet "cells," but not able to develop traditional software logic.

3. Customer partner list

   This item is a listing of the customers that are willing to actively participate in the development effort being started. If there is not a clear definition of the type of user of the system or there are not customers of this type willing to actively participate in the development, the chances of success are greatly reduced. After all, how can you supply a product to fill a demand if you don't understand the demand? Without customer commitment, key milestones in the process, such as the analysis phase requirements specification deliverable, will not be possible.

4.2.2 Activities

ANALYSIS STEPS

1. Write use cases.
2. Verify use cases with customers.
3. Extract and document requirements from use cases.
4. Extract nouns from use cases.
   a. Associate verbs from use cases with nouns.
5. Identify and document application classes from the noun list.
   a. Identify and document responsibilities from the verb list.
6. Walk through use cases, using the identified application classes.
   a. Draw message flow diagrams (optional).
   b. Expand responsibilities as needed.
   c. Add new classes as needed.
7. Prototype use cases.
8. Verify the prototype with customers.
   a. Functionality.
   b. User interface.
9. Update use cases and requirements as needed.
10. Iterate steps 7 through 9 for areas that don't have solid requirements.

> **11.** Document customer requirements.
> **12.** Document the draft system architecture.
> **13.** Document the draft user's manual.

See Chapter 3, "O-O Development Methodology," for detailed discussions of the steps and their deliverables.

4.2.2.1 Write use cases

An important input to the analysis phase is a list of customers willing to work with the development team to build the product. Documenting the customers' requirements obviously requires some customers to find out what their requirements are.

It is possible that if enough effort has been put into the draft requirements document that some work can be done before talking directly to customers. However, the assessment period of the IDP will require that customers actively review what has been done.

The first activity should be to actively work with customers that you are targeting your new product for. Hold discussions with the customers about their needs. Ask probing questions to make sure you get at their real needs and that you uncover as much as possible. Everyone has lots of wants—try to go just beyond what is needed and separate the needs into priorities. Document the conversations (tape recording may help). The intent is for one use case to detail one major user function.

The actual words used are important—you want to model the *customers'* application, not yours. The terms should be the customers' terms all the way to the product. That's what real-world modeling is all about. Write down what you heard the users say the system should do in descriptive text scenarios (the use cases). While use cases are not absolutely required, they are helpful in making sure effective communication is taking place (specifications are much more dry). They are also good inputs for test cases and the user manual.

4.2.2.2 Verify use cases with customers

Go over the new system scenarios with the users, making any changes necessary. Make sure you understand the *intent* of what the system is to do. The underlying intent is what will become the requirements—

the *what* of the system. The *how* will change constantly—the *what* will not.

> ## FUNCTION VERIFICATION— BALANCE INQUIRY
>
> *(Analyst)* The *balance inquiry* function will get the customer's account information and then give the customer a receipt with the account number and current balance printed on it. Is that what is needed for this function?
>
> *(A Customer)* It sounds pretty good, but I'd word the message differently than you showed me. I'd want it to say "Pick your type of account" rather than just showing the names of the types of accounts to choose from. The content is good—it needs to have a date on the receipt though.
>
> *(Analyst)* That's good information about the message, but realize that it may change in the final design. The new requirement I'm hearing is that the *date must appear on a balance request receipt.* Is that right?
>
> *(A Customer)* That's right—I have to see the date, so I can remember when I got the balance. I may have multiple receipts in my pocket, looking at my checkbook a few days later.

Make sure that you and your customer are clear about the terms being used. Donald Gause walks through detailed exercises to make sure you are communicating effectively.[2] A couple of points from his book:

- Reword a requirement and feed it back to the customer, asking for verification of your understanding.
- Explain terms and notation used in your design diagrams if you use them in discussions with your customer.

4.2.2.3 Extract and document requirements from use cases

Pull out the underlying requirements from the scenarios (an example of this step is shown in Section 3.2.1, "Write Use Cases"). Be specific—avoid vague phrases that are subject to interpretation, such as "quick response" (one-half second? two seconds? five minutes?). The requirements are the functional and informational needs of *what* the system is to provide, and not *how* the system is to provide it. Try

---

[2]Donald C. Gause and Gerald M. Weinberg, *Exploring Requirements: Quality Before Design* (New York: Dorset House Publishing Co., Inc., 1989), pp. 103, 127.

to get an estimate of the priority of each requirement from the customers and put the requirements into the draft detailed requirements specification.

4.2.2.4 Extract nouns from use cases

Look for salient nouns in the text. Think about implied types of objects when the passive voice is used. List the nouns.

List attribute words related to the nouns, such as discussions of *name* for a customer. A customer's name may not be something that is key to the application, but must nevertheless be kept with the customer objects.

> **Note:** Key nouns and verbs are highlighted in the ATM use cases shown in Appendix D. "Complete ATM Application."

ASSOCIATE VERBS FROM USE CASES WITH NOUNS: Look for verb phrases that are used with nouns. List the verb phrases with the appropriate nouns.

4.2.2.5 Identify and document application classes
from the noun list

Go over the noun list, identifying classes for those nouns that are important to the application being built. Throw out extraneous nouns.

Computer novices can be useful here, since they focus on the *problem* domain. Since they have no computer background, the solution domain is not likely to affect their view of the real world being modeled. The problem is that professional programmers can't help but "jump ahead" to "code in their head."

For example, looking at the list from the initial ATM requirements, we see that *money* is in the list. While it is certainly important that funds are being manipulated by our ATM application, perhaps the money could be modeled as a floating-point number, which is a base system class, rather than a new ATM application class.

Describe the newly identified classes. Maintain traceability to the requirements derived from the use case. Other attributes of the nouns should be noted as state data for the classes (an example might be a *balance* for an *account*).

IDENTIFY AND DOCUMENT RESPONSIBILITIES FROM THE VERB LIST: Go over the verb list for a new class and document related method names and descriptions. Maintain traceability to the requirements derived from the use case.

> ## SAVINGSACCOUNT VERB AND RESPONSIBILITIES LIST
>
> | VERB PHRASE | RESPONSIBILITY |
> |---|---|
> | *move money* | transfer:from: to: |
> | *withdraw cash* | withdraw: |
> | *deposit money* | deposit: |
> | *get balance* | balance |

Note: Activities after this step will assign the *transfer:from: to:* to the *TransferTransaction* class. Also, some of the methods such as *deposit:* will move to the *Account* class, which is the superclass of the *Savings-Account* class. The *Account* class is an abstract class that allows the specific account classes to share common methods and state data.

4.2.2.6 *Walk through use cases, using the application classes*

The analysts step through the use cases, discussing what the classes would do to provide the required functions. Customers should probably not be involved in this step, since they will not be concerned with the prototype design of the classes. They will be involved again when there is a prototype to view.

The analysts should be asking themselves the question: "Do we understand the types of objects in the system?" This will require some rudimentary level of competency in the problem domain. When our project first started, we spent a few intense days discussing the system requirements, postulating what types of objects were there, changing them, discussing scenarios some more, et cetera. It certainly helped that we had an O-O design expert helping us, since we knew what we wanted and believed in O-O, but didn't know at the time how to go about a good O-O analysis.

> ## USE CASE WALKTHROUGH— BALANCE INQUIRY
>
> *(Analyst 1)* The *balanceInquiry* message would then go to the *Atm* class, which would then create a *BalanceInquiry* transaction object instance. The transaction object would then ask its *Customer* class object for its list of accounts.
> *(Analyst 2)* But wait a second . . . we don't have a method in any of the transaction classes that gives us the requesting customer

object! Maybe instead of using a generic "new" for the transaction, we could have a *createFor:* method that got the customer object as a parameter.
(Analyst 1)   Agreed—I'll add it to the list.

DRAW MESSAGE FLOW DIAGRAMS (OPTIONAL): Document the message
flows between the classes in order to provide the required end user
functions. These flows are useful to document the system design for
understanding. The flows should focus on *application* level flows, and
not every flow.

EXPAND RESPONSIBILITIES AS NEEDED: Document additional or modified responsibilities for the classes that are discovered as a part of the
use-case walkthrough.

ADD NEW CLASSES AS NEEDED: Document additional classes that are
discovered as a part of the use-case walkthrough.

4.2.2.7 Prototype use cases

In the prototyping language, model the current understanding of the
system for one or more use cases. A new focus is on collaboration concerns. Ask questions such as: "Do I need a relationship between these
classes?" This will help architect the contracts between classes. Remember to keep the right responsibilities with the right classes, based
on where they would be in the real world.

The focus in developing the prototype is effective communication
with the users. The prototype should have very loose performance requirements. The IDP emphasis is on delivering functions in relatively
short time periods, with demonstrations to customers. Feedback from
the customers is immediately fed into the short planning for the next
iteration.

During the assessment, the requirements are updated. During
the prototyping, it is important to look for existing components to reuse. Rapid turnaround is important—purity and performance are not
as important at this time. The reuse library is a good place to look for
domain-specific components. As the reuse library grows, this will provide more and more of a quick-start capability, during both analysis
and design.

Develop UI classes to allow the user to drive the model classes.
Work with your usability group to get the design of these classes right,
from an ease-of-use and UI requirements standpoint.

4.2.2.8 Verify the prototype with customers

Show the prototype to the users, discussing what functions and information are provided. Find out which requirements are *most important* by watching users' reactions. By finding out early what is not needed, you can save time and money. You will also find out what must be rethought.

FUNCTIONALITY: Verify the required functionality, noting any differences from the requirements and use cases as they currently stand.

The customer will certainly want to add function "on the fly." Watch out! "Feature creep" will eat you alive—keep the focus on the key requirements. I suggest revisiting important requirements when you get pressure for more functions, putting them in perspective and allowing the customers to realize the trade-offs. Offer to put additional items on a list for the *next* release.

USER INTERFACE: The usability group will verify the user interface requirements that specifically apply to the application, such as certain information being provided together or other information being accessible from certain types of fields being presented. Avoid making too many UI requirements, which will lock too much of the "how" of the design in too early and result in change management problems.

ITERATE FOR AREAS THAT DON'T HAVE SOLID REQUIREMENTS: Return to Section 4.2.2.6, "Walk through use cases, using the application classes," continuing the prototyping effort for the use cases that need further clarification. Areas that have feasibility risks may also need more iterations.

4.2.2.9 Update use cases and requirements as needed

The requirements document is *the* key deliverable of the analysis phase and must be maintained. The use cases are inputs to the test phase for test cases and to information development for the user manual, and therefore should be updated.

4.2.2.10 Document customer requirements

Once the prototype iterations have taken place, a final requirements document must be created from the documentation that has been gathered. This is the overall intent of the analysis phase—to generate a *validated* detailed requirements document.

This is the most important deliverable of this phase. In fact, the design and test phase (Section 4.3, "Design and Test Phase") cannot begin without this deliverable.

Obviously, all deliverables are important, or we wouldn't bother with them at all. It's just that some are more important than others.

For example, the identification of key types of objects that exist in the architecture draft gives the designers a good start at understanding the application. However, if this draft is incomplete, the design and test phase could start, if necessary. Without clear requirements though, there is no sense in wasting time designing the wrong system.

4.2.2.11 Document the draft system architecture

Once the analysis phase is complete, documentation of the classes, methods, subsystems, and contracts will carry forward to the design and test phase as *draft* documentation. The designers are free to change the design (but will nonetheless benefit from what has been done).

4.2.2.12 Document the draft user's manual

The use cases are key inputs to the user manual, which should be passed on to the design and test phase in the form of a draft user manual. The information development group should be the owners and writers of this document, in coordination with the software development team.

4.2.3 Deliverables

The analysis phase has the following deliverables:

1. Detailed requirements specification

    The requirements specification concentrates on the functions needed by the users of the system. The end-user functions are discussed in terms of *what* is to be done, and not *how* it is to be done. For example, "Hard-copy printouts of the xyz report shall be possible" is a functional requirement, while "Hard-copy printouts of xyz reports will be from the *File* pulldown" has design mixed in with the function. There are times when requirements specifications will contain information that would normally be considered design. For example, if the user requires that there be screen layouts or navigation in a certain way, for historical or training or other reasons, this could be a part of the requirements, even though UI concerns are normally part of design. An outline for the requirements specification is shown in Appendix E, "Requirements Specification Outline."

    The central portion of the requirements are:
    a. The functional requirements.

    Remember that areas such as UI design are usually *not* a requirement, but rather design.

b. The customer type.

While this was an input to this effort, it should be documented in the requirements document.

c. The target language and hardware.

The analysis prototype may be done in any language and hardware configuration, since this prototype will not evolve into the final product (the design iterations evolve into the product).

2. System architecture draft

This includes a definition of the key classes in the system and the architected interfaces (contracts) for the key classes. It also may include, depending on system size, an identification of subsystems. This is a draft and its content is ultimately the property and responsibility of the designers. This document is meant to capture information learned during the analysis phase, but not to make it difficult to change. The designers own the architecture and design of the system. The analysts key on requirements. These will often be the same people, filling different roles.

3. User manual draft

This is an example of the desired user interface. It is up to the designers, working with usability, to decide the presentation specifics. This UI is intended to capture the information gained through working with the users. While this is good information that should not be lost, changes to the UI need to be easy. Requirements are documented and controlled through a change process and are therefore not easy to modify.

4. Throwaway prototype code

You must resist the temptation to evolve from the analysis prototype. The main reason is that the code was a "quick and dirty" effort, geared toward rapidly trying things out and presenting them to users. There is no focus on creating good reusable abstractions. There is little focus on tuning performance (unless it becomes unusable). There is no organized testing. This is all alright if the goals and deliverables of the different phases are not confused or misused. The process is there—trust it and yourselves and don't get into panic mode or let management pressure you into "shipping the prototype."

You do eventually ship the design "prototype." It is not really a prototype in the true sense of the word, though. In analysis, you are truly prototyping a "mock-up" of the system. It's probably largely made up of band-aids, smoke and mirrors, and chewing gum. The design-phase code iterates, evolving into the desired product.

4.3 DESIGN AND TEST PHASE

The design and test phase uses an iterative development technique to develop subsystems. The code evolves into the final product code, with emphasis during iterations correspondingly changed from the analysis phase.

The IDP iterations will be longer than during the analysis phase. Three to four month iterations will be typical, with moderate planning and assessment periods and a long production period. The designer must be careful to make sure that the efforts stay focused on delivering the requirements in a final product.

Scheduling will be driven by the detailed requirements from the analysis phase. The design is still exploratory, trying different ways to most effectively meet the requirements. Functions should be scheduled for a number of iterations based on the complexity of the item, with more iterations planned for more complex pieces of the system. This allows time to get feedback and to hit implementation "walls" for areas such as the user interface and time critical code.

The emphasis during the IDP production period is on developing complete functionality for the next iteration of a system function, for input to the assessment period. Customers are still involved during the assessment period. The IDP assessment period of the major iterations are now emphasizing performance, reuse, and quality. It is not that the analysis phase ignored these areas, but that the emphasis shifts. In analysis, for example, it might be acceptable to have ten-second response times for some system functions being demonstrated. In the design and test phase, this would not be acceptable and plans to improve the performance would be incorporated into the schedule for the next major iteration.

Multiple iterations of the development methodology are followed for each subsystem. These iterations can occur in parallel or serially, depending on the strategy followed and the subsystem interdependencies.

Figure 4.5 shows the prerequisites and deliverables for the design and test phase, which are discussed in the following sections.

4.3.1 Design Overview

In doing an O-O design, you want to focus on the types of objects in the problem domain first. You have a good start at this in the analysis-

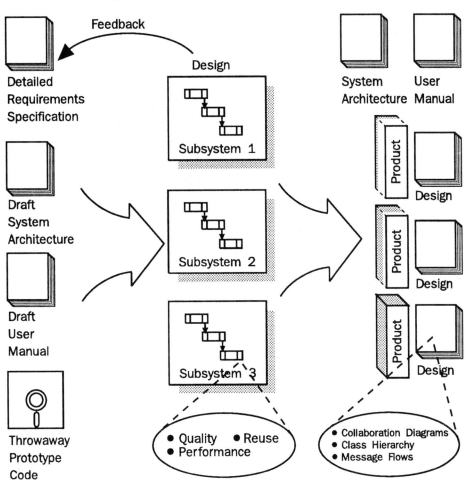

Figure 4.5   Design-Phase Prerequisites and Deliverables

phase deliverables. The focus is on creating new business classes and reusing existing business classes in a new configuration. The latter "bottom-up" leverage of previous work should become more and more common as you contribute classes to the reuse library with each project.

Tom Love has suggested that design "patterns" of loose, coordinated guidelines be followed rather than strict rules.[3] The use of patterns is based on similar concepts being used in urban planning and allows for flexibility while achieving overall goals. You can base your

---

[3]Tom Love, "Timeless Design of Information Systems," *Object Magazine*, (November/December 1991), pp. 42–48.

project's guidelines on those discussed in this book, modifying them as you gain experience.

The objects being worked on will be model objects as well as UI objects. The goal is to focus on the model objects first and the UI objects last. Part of the reason for this is that the *required functions* are what is important. If good model object classes for your business are developed, many different types of user interfaces can be used with those same objects *without modification!* That is the rest of the reason—you want to keep the UI and non-UI (model) object classes independent, to maintain high reuse (see Figure 4.6).

The model and UI portions of the application should be loosely coupled, with different UIs possibly being used with a single set of model objects for your business.

The design information should be maintained along with the object implementation. This has, of course, always been the dream of software development, but seldom the waking reality. In the case of

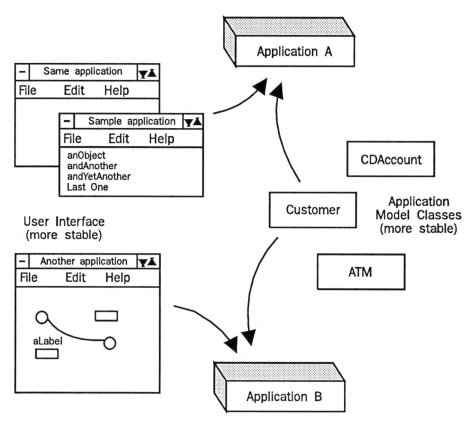

Figure 4.6 Model and UI Portions of an O-O Application

objects, though, the design information can be associated with the objects that are developed. This is one of the key requirements for tools that support the process and methodology.

4.3.2 Test Overview

Figure 4.7 depicts a suggested test strategy for an O-O system.

The basic idea is that you want to focus your testing on one class at a time. You want to test the classes in a *bottom-up* fashion. By that, I mean that whenever possible you want to run a test with only one unverified piece—the class being verified. To do that, you use base system classes (which are assumed to be verified) and your application classes that have been previously verified. This implies that lower-level application classes will be tested first, since they will depend al-

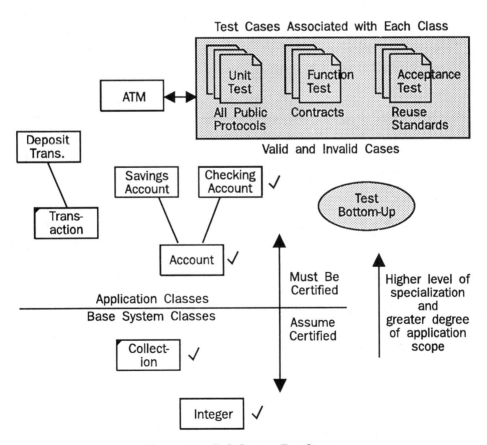

Figure 4.7 O-O System Test Strategy

most entirely upon the base classes. By *lower level,* I mean that they do not comprise a large amount of application function, which would imply utilization of other application classes. These classes with less application scope and fewer interclass dependencies (couplings) are easier to test using only other classes that have been verified. There may certainly be cases where you cannot test a class in conjunction with verified classes only. In these cases, you will have to violate your basic strategy—just keep this in mind when you are viewing the test results and searching for any culprits to problems encountered. When you have to use two or more unverified classes together, look at the class couplings to make sure they are necessary.

You need to test superclasses *before* subclasses, since the subclasses inherit behavior "up" the hierarchy. An exception to this is *abstract* classes, which cannot be directly tested, since they never have any instances. I would suggest that the first subclass tested be required to exercise all common behaviors, if possible. If the subclass can't be used to exercise 100 percent of the behavior of the superclass, you may want to reconsider the inheritance relationship.

This strategy maximizes the likelihood that a problem encountered during testing is due to errors in the targeted class, and not some collaborating class.

Cheatham suggests that you look at the message flows between classes in the system and that you focus first on the "sinks"—the classes that do not collaborate further with other application classes.[4] I believe that the intent of this strategy is the same as that proposed here. If looking at message flow threads helps you to choose class test orders that simplify testing, then use this technique.

The testing that takes place during the design phase iterates along with the code under development, as shown in Figure 4.8.

The goal of testing as discussed in this document is to verify that the *requirements* are being met. The *design* is not tested, per se. After all, a certain implementation is not required, but is one of many ways to meet the documented user requirements. The design is certainly an input for the testers' understanding, but it is a *tool* requirement that the integrity between any implementation and design documentation (such as collaboration diagrams) be maintained. Focusing on requirements reduces the probability that design changes will ripple through the test cases.

---

[4]Thomas J. Cheatham and Lee Mellinger, "Testing Object-Oriented Software Systems," *ACM 18th Annual Computer Science Conference Proceedings,* 1990, pp. 161–65.

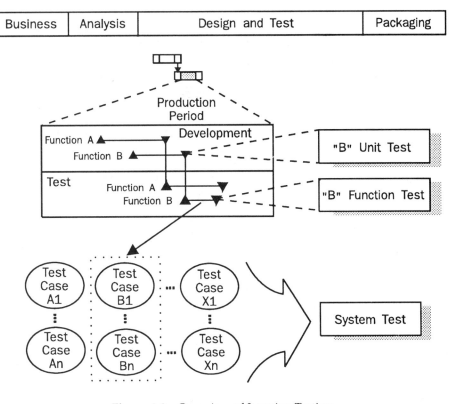

Figure 4.8   Overview of Iterative Testing

As shown in Figure 4.8, the developers are responsible to *unit* test their own functional line item code. The developers write and run test cases against the classes being developed in order to complete their unit testing. You should *expect to write as much or more test code as production code.* For example, Marc Rettig reports that 18 percent of the code written on his project was production code, while 35 percent was test procedure code![5] His team spent about one half the amount of time per line of test code as production code, so the net result is that they spent about the same amount of time writing code to test their system as they did writing the system itself. Plan time for this necessary effort.

---

[5]Marc Rettig, "Testing Made Palatable," *Communications of the ACM*, 34, No. 5 (May 1991), 25–29.

A single test case is targeted toward a *single* class. This is the basic unit of a test. Other classes are certainly exercised, via messages, by a test case run against the targeted class. For UI classes, the tests can exercise large portions of the system. This type of test would typically occur later in the testing, building on previously tested application classes (see Section 4.3.2, "Test Overview").

Figure 4.9 shows the basic contents of a test case. There are two basic kinds of test cases:

1. batch: These test cases exercise the model classes and can be run without developer or tester intervention.

2. interactive: These test cases exercise the UI of the application.

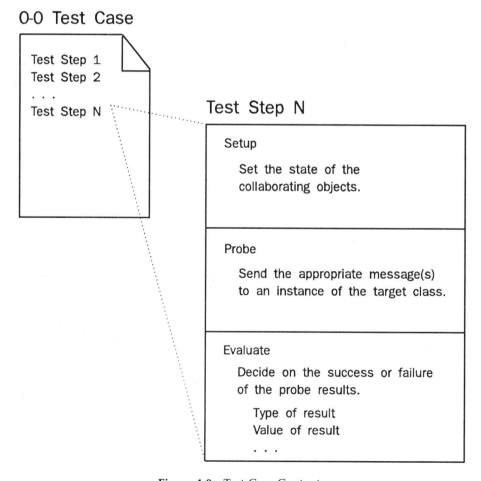

Figure 4.9 Test Case Contents

The test case is made up of *test steps,* which are themselves comprised of *setup, probe,* and *evaluate* portions. The *setup* portion prepares the testbed for the class by setting the state of collaborating classes and the test class itself so that the test can run. The *probe* portion sends the proper message(s) to the class being tested. The *evaluate* portion compares the expected result with the actual result of the probe. For example, a *BalanceInquiry* test case might have test steps that set and check balance values for each of the different types of accounts.

As weekly build-cycle drivers become available (see Appendix G, "Build Cycle"), the testers run preliminary *function* tests. The function test cases iterate along with the line item, generating a number of variations to exercise boundary conditions, valid cases, and invalid cases as the code evolves. The final, formal set of the function tests comprehensively make up the *system* test. It is recommended that an independent group of testers be used during system test to fully exercise the system. A more extensive form of unit testing is performed for those pieces of code that are candidates for the reuse library (see Section 4.3.2.2, "Reuse Library Testing").

Figure 4.10 compares traditional with iterative verification.

In the figure, you can see that traditionally testing had a long delay time to verify the "predictions" contained in the specifications. Using the iterative technique, testing closely follows function delivery and itself iterates on test cases, while more immediately giving development outside feedback for work recently delivered.

Figure 4.11 shows sources of information for test case development. The ultimate source is the requirements specification, since this is the "purchase contract" for the system.

4.3.2.1 Iterative testing

The goals for using iterative testing are:[6]

1. **To minimize the impacts to tests from development changes**
   Due to the iterative nature of development using the IDP, changes to tests are going to be fast and frequent. Testing needs to iterate in a similar manner for its activities.

2. **To reduce development cycle time**
   Rapid feedback to development throughout the effort allows impacts of errors to be reduced, thereby shortening the overall cycle time.

---

[6]These are adapted from discussions with Kevin Haga.

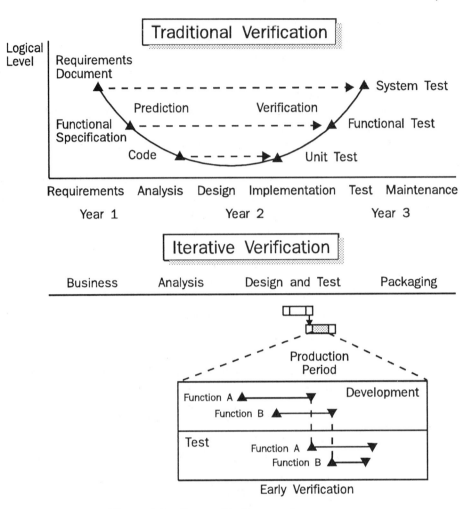

Figure 4.10 System Verification Comparison

The deliverables specific to the relationship between the development and test teams during the design and test phase are shown in Figure 4.12.[7]

Development gives the test team build-code and line-item status reports for each week's builds. Test then returns any problems that are found in the form of an *intra*departmental problem report. These reports are processed in a less formal, low-overhead fashion. More formal reports will come later.

---

[7]Adapted from discussions with Kevin Haga.

Test Case Development

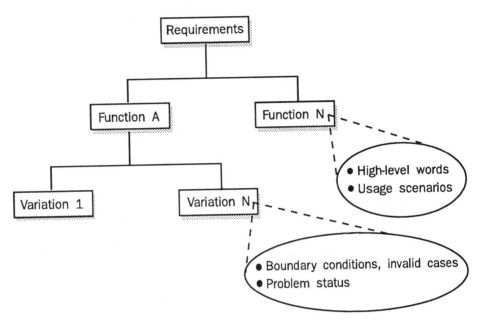

Figure 4.11   Source Information for Testing

4.3.2.2 Reuse library testing

More extensive "unit" testing of classes (more accurately called *acceptance* testing) occurs when they are "complete." It is at this time that abstractions are again looked for and created, if possible. These abstractions will reduce your volume of code. I have seen it time and again on our projects that code volume drops as the design is cleaned up, abstractions are pulled out, and responsibilities are moved to the correct class. It is not uncommon for twelve line methods to be reduced to one line.

Flexibility can be built in at this time, as well as performing any cleanup or documentation required. The abstractions and robust classes that result are candidates for the company's reuse library of building blocks. Once in the library, the "certified" code is available for company-wide use. It is not recommended to reuse code outside the project that is not in the reuse library. This primarily has to do with stability of the code, ownership, documentation, and support. It will undermine your reuse efforts if first-time users get components

Iterative Testing

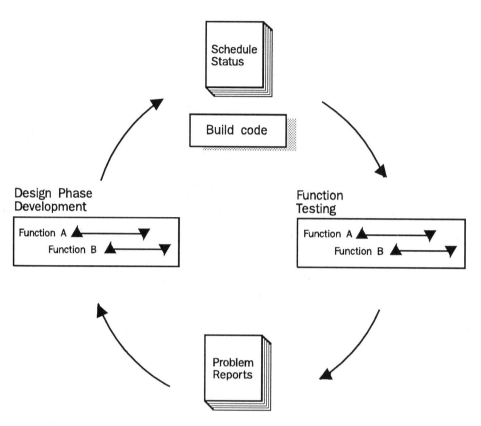

Figure 4.12   Development—Test Team Iteration Deliverables

that do not work. The only thing worse than bugs in *your* code is bugs in someone *else's* code!

The abstractions may be created by the class programmers instead of the application programmers. The class programmers are more likely to discover abstractions, since they are exposed to a wider range of applications. See Appendix F, "Development Team Roles," for a discussion of development teams and roles.

Acceptance of reusable components into the reuse library should be based on certain criteria:

1. Documentation
   a. Description (including restrictions)
   b. Interface (calling sequence and parameters)
   c. Keywords (for categorization in the library)

    d. Prerequisites (operating system and other)
    e. Example use and results (e.g., test cases)
2. Suitability for reuse
    a. Provides a complete function
    b. Has a parameterized interface
    c. Has applicability across multiple problem domains
3. Robustness
    a. Passes an acceptance test of its function

4.3.2.3 Problem tracking

Tracking problems is important both during and after development. The concentration of problems in a particular class signals a need to redesign and/or reimplement the class. It can also signal the fact that the class has new requirements (contracts) that are not being met.

    The tracking system should be integrated into the development system and have granularity to all levels. See Appendix H.2, "Problem Report Requirements," for detailed requirements for a problem-reporting system.

4.3.3 Prerequisites

The design and test phase has the following prerequisites:

1. *Detailed requirements specification:* This is absolutely required in order to start the design. While there may be some leeway with other prerequisites, there is none here.
2. *System architecture draft:* This draft documents *key classes, contracts,* and *subsystems* that were used for the analysis prototype.
3. *User's manual draft:* This draft contains the *user interface* information that was gathered during the analysis phase.
4. *Throwaway analysis prototype:* This is the throwaway prototype code used to perform the system analysis. It was developed with the analysis deliverables (e.g., requirements document) in mind, and not the design deliverables (e.g., product code).

4.3.4 Activities

```
──────────────────── DESIGN STEPS ────────────────────


  1. Produce a development plan.
  2. Review the analysis-phase deliverables.
       a. Validate the architecture draft.
```

   b. Expand responsibilities as needed.
   c. Add new classes as needed.
3. Document the target language, hardware, and software platforms.
4. Search the reuse library for applicable off-the-shelf components.
5. Look for overlap of responsibilities, similarity of types of objects.
   a. Create application mini-hierarchies.
6. Draw collaboration diagrams.
   a. Identify and document subsystems.
   b. Identify and document contracts.
7. Draw message flow diagrams.
8. Walk through the design diagrams and documentation.
   a. Expand responsibilities as needed.
   b. Add new classes as needed.
9. Implement subsystems.
   a. Look for abstractions.
   b. Write methods.
   c. Unit test classes.
   d. Function test classes.
   e. Assess performance, quality, reusability.
10. Iterate step 9 for areas that don't meet requirements.
11. Test subsystems.
12. Document final subsystem designs.
13. Document final architecture.
14. Document final user's manual.
15. System test the complete system.

4.3.4.1 Produce a development plan

This is not much different than any other development. The idea is to lay out the line items to be worked on and collect schedule information. The difference is that the line items have multiple iterations (see Appendix H, "Sample Line Item Schedule and Description") and the schedules have flexibility built in, via the IDP feedback (see Chapter 2, "Iterative Development Process.")

For large systems, break the problem into subsystems early in the project at low cohesion and message-traffic points. Then control the interfaces between the subsystems via contracts. This will allow development of the subsystems relatively independently. If the interfaces are not stable, you will suffer. On our project, we had major changes in the interface to our graphics system in the middle of development of graphics editors built on top of this framework. Needless to say, this was a time of significant pain for the editor developers (I know—I had the most complex graphical editor at the time). In this case, we did not work in parallel across points of low cohesion—on the contrary, the editors were deeply involved in driving the requirements for the graphics base that was being developed in parallel.

4.3.4.2 Review the Analysis-Phase Deliverables

Make sure the design team understands the requirements. Review the analysis prototype (*demonstration* not implementation). Review the UI requirements.

1. **Validate the architecture draft.** Review the classes, responsibilities, and any subsystems that were defined.
2. **Expand responsibilities as needed.** Document additional or modified responsibilities for the classes that are discovered as a part of the design walkthrough.
3. **Add new classes as needed.** Document additional classes that are discovered as a part of the design walkthrough. In particular, pay attention to implementation-specific areas, such as device-related and target-platform classes, since these would not have been focused on during the analysis phase.

4.3.4.3 Document the target language, hardware, and software platforms

These will be decided implicitly or explicitly by the requirements. These issues will certainly affect your design. For example, if you decide to use C++, the class libraries available will be different from those available in Smalltalk. Also, C++ opens up the option of using multiple inheritance in your design, which Smalltalk does not support.

One area to keep an eye on is emerging standards. For example, the Object Management Group, a consortium of companies working on object technology standards, has developed a common distributed object architecture.[8]

---

[8]Richard Soley, ''Combined ORB Submission Completed,'' *First Class*, (September/October 1991), p. 5.

4.3.4.4 *Search the reuse library for applicable off-the-shelf components*

The focus is now on building the real system. There may be solid components in the company's reuse library, which is stocked by previous projects' classes, applications, and tools. It is helpful if there is a "roving expert" available for key topics for a project. For example, if there is a need in a banking application for communications between sites and ATM machines, you would like to have someone with applicable skills on your team. What we are trying to do on our projects is to rotate people with key skills through a "roving expert" position, where they would go to one or two projects for a few months, to help the project get off the ground. The experts would own and "carry with them" a set of components that relates to the area of expertise. There are a couple of benefits to this:

1. The project obviously benefits from the expertise.
2. The reusable components improve, since they are used in a new situation.

Good reusable components do not happen the first time they are developed. They happen through ownership and *usage*. Having an expert own components related to key technical topics and use them on different projects will help achieve the goal of a reuse library stocked with good reusable components.

Keep statistics on searches that failed, searches that succeeded, and actual *uses* of components (such as through a follow-up inquiry to a requestor). See Appendix I, "Measurements and Metrics," for more details.

The design should take into account the existing designs of the company's frameworks (groups of classes that provide some functions) and individual reusable classes in the reuse library in order to reuse them effectively. If you don't design for reuse, you will not have reuse. Target classes to contribute to the reuse library.

4.3.4.5 *Look for overlap of responsibilities, similarity of types of objects*

Overlap of responsibilities and similar object types indicate a missing abstract class and/or subclassing possibilities. For example, we found many overlaps in the responsibilities for *Account, SavingsAccount,* and *CheckingAccount.* Since these are similar types of objects, this is a good indication that there is an application inheritance mini-hierarchy needed between these classes. Either one of these classes is a superclass of the others, or there is an abstract class that can be created to facilitate sharing of code between similar classes. In this example, *Account* is a superclass of the other specializations of an account.

If classes with overlap of responsibilities are not similar in type, then they will not have a subclass-superclass relationship. Remember, the class inheritance hierarchy is intended for "is-a" type relationships (such as, a *savingsAccount* is-a type of *account*). It is possible that our system has a *bank* object, which holds a collection of *account* objects. You may be tempted to subclass *OrderedCollection*, since you could use its methods to manipulate the list of accounts. However, a *bank* has other attributes, such as name, that an *orderedCollection* does not. What you really want to do in this case is to have the *bank* hold an orderedCollection of accounts.

CREATE APPLICATION MINI-HIERARCHIES: Application abstract classes and subclass relationships in general form hierarchies within some of the classes in the application. These hierarchies (and the other classes) will have to be optimally placed in the overall class inheritance hierarchy (see Section 3.2.4, "Place Classes in the Inheritance Hierarchy").

4.3.4.6 Draw collaboration diagrams

Collaboration diagrams give the developer a place to visualize the classes involved in a piece of the system, as well as their interactions. The key pieces shown are:

1. Subsystems
2. Classes
3. Subclasses
4. Contracts
5. Contract usages

Through viewing these class groupings and relationships, the design of the system (versus just the design of the classes) becomes apparent. As you begin to build up some classes, placing them on collaboration diagrams, you can pictorially start to see groupings of interdependent classes and services being provided between these groupings. Other views at lower levels of detail such as class and subsystem cards (Figure 3.7 and Figure 3.9), are available. Information access for much of the methodology steps can take many forms, from paper to on-line tools. If on-line tools are available, they should provide the most efficient, direct access to the objects, for example by mouse actions.

The notation used in the collaboration diagrams is as documented in *Designing Object-Oriented Software* by Rebecca Wirfs-Brock et al.

> **Note:** Contained objects can be shown or hidden, based on details needed for the diagram. For example, a subsystem can appear as a single box with only its name and contracts shown.

IDENTIFY AND DOCUMENT SUBSYSTEMS: The clusters of more tightly coupled classes should be grouped in a higher-level whole, called a subsystem. Name the subsystem by the overall function being provided. For example, an ATM system may have *account management* and *interface* subsystems, providing account and equipment functions, respectively. If you cannot name the subsystem, you need to reexamine the clustering. Remove any classes that do not belong.

Treat the subsystems as functionally cohesive "black boxes" that can be developed relatively independently. This may be done in the analysis phase for large systems in order to manage the complexity. A small application may only have one subsystem. Subsystems may be reused from the reuse library.

IDENTIFY AND DOCUMENT CONTRACTS: Look at the requests coming into the new subsystems. They will become the public protocols, or contracts, to the encapsulated subsystem.

For example, the *Account* class naturally has methods that relate to managing the different types of customer accounts. These methods can be grouped into a public, supported contract called *Manage account balances*, as shown in the following box.

ACCOUNT CLASS

     Description—The *Account* class is an abstract class that provides common services for all types of bank accounts.
     Superclasses—*PersistentObject*
     Subclasses—*SavingsAccount, CheckingAccount*

CONTRACTS

1. [1] Manage account balances is implemented by the following public method(s):
   a. withdraw:
   b. deposit:
   c. balance

RESPONSIBILITY	DESCRIPTION
balance	Return my current balance.
balance: anAmount.	(Private) Set my current balance to anAmount.

deposit: anAmount	Add anAmount to my currentBalance.
withdraw: anAmount	Subtract anAmount from my current-bBalance.
DATA	**DESCRIPTION**
currentBalance	The amount of funds I currently hold.
withdrawalLimit	The amount of funds that can currently be withdrawn from me.

4.3.4.7 Draw message flow diagrams

Message flow diagrams (Figure 3.3) are useful to visualize the types of requests that a subsystem, class, and method will receive. The message flows are typically created based on use-cases developed earlier. They can, however, be drawn based on other inputs, such as requirements documents. The flows are design documentation that span subsystem, class, and method implementations.

4.3.4.8 Walk through the design diagrams and documentation

Look for abstractions that can be gleaned from similar classes. Examine the placement of responsibilities, making sure that the methods in a class fit well with the type of object it represents.

You may want to talk through the use-case scenarios with your team. Software development is still, in part, an art form. It has been helpful in our efforts to have interaction between the team members with different viewpoints to end up with the optimum design. This also fosters buy-in through participation.

EXPAND RESPONSIBILITIES AS NEEDED: Document additional or modified responsibilities for the classes that are discovered as a part of the design walkthrough.

ADD NEW CLASSES AS NEEDED: Document additional classes that are discovered as a part of the design walkthrough. In particular, pay attention to implementation-specific areas, such as device-related and target-platform classes.

4.3.4.9 Implement subsystems

The decomposition of the system into subsystems is primarily for filtering of information. This is not a new concept. Dataflow diagrams (DFDs) have used decomposition levels for functions for a number of years. The idea with subsystems is to group functionally cohesive classes together and control the interface to them from a client's perspective. The controlled interfaces are called *contracts.* The subsystems are connected via the defined contracts only. Subsystems can be treated as black boxes from other subsystems.

In building the subsystems, which should be loosely coupled with other subsystems, the design and implementation efforts can be scheduled serially or in parallel, depending on factors such as resource availability. During the development of each of the subsystems, the IDP is used. Major iterations are scheduled, line items on the schedule are started using the O-O methodology steps (Chapter 3, "O-O Development Methodology") and weekly build cycles (Appendix G, "Build Cycle"), and testing of delivered components is performed as the pieces are submitted for the build.

The focus is now on *reuse, performance,* and *quality* of the software, since this code will evolve into the final product.

LOOK FOR ABSTRACTIONS: These will greatly help with the application implementation and are prime candidates for the reuse library. For example, when we first identified possible responsibilities for the different candidate classes, it was apparent that those listed for the different types of accounts overlapped.

─────────────── **ATM VERB LIST** ───────────────

NOUN	ASSOCIATED VERBS
savingsAccount	moveMoney
	withdrawCash
	depositMoney
	getBalance
checkingAccount	moveMoney
	withdrawCash
	depositMoney
	getBalance
account	moveMoney
	withdrawCash
	depositMoney
	getBalance

We can pull out the common responsibilities into the abstract *Account* class. An *Account* class may not have even been identified at this time, in which case the developer would create the abstract class when he or she noticed the overlap in function and type for the *CheckingAccount* and *SavingsAccount* classes.

Don't get too hung up on subclassing. As Figure 4.13 shows, the hierarchy is not typically extremely deep.[9] These numbers are based on a moderate-to-large Smalltalk application hierarchy. Subclassing only goes so far. Most of the volume of classes in your applications (other than when you are building frameworks) will use collaborating relationships across the hierarchy.

WRITE METHODS: The previous work-to list and describe class responsibilities as well as any message flow diagrams that were developed should make writing code for methods relatively straightforward.

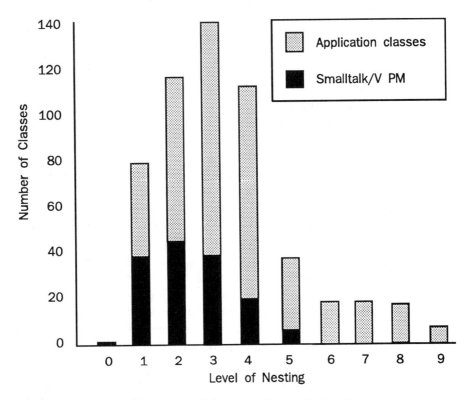

Figure 4.13 Inheritance Hierarchy Depth

---

[9]This figure is from Mark Lorenz, "Real World Reuse," *Journal of Object-Oriented Programming (JOOP)* (November/December 1991) p. 35, and is based on an actual project's class hierarchy.

Cardinality relationships will help make decisions about necessary instance variables and whether the variables should hold collections of objects or a single object.

In developing the code, the reuse library components should be used whenever possible, since they are solid, existing building blocks. Rewards should be built into the company's appraisal system to encourage reuse.

The choice of language should come *after* documenting the requirements and finding the right classes in the problem domain. The language choice should be the best one to meet those requirements while modeling the solution using objects. Modeling the objects will certainly be easier with an O-O language and environment. The question is: What parts of the system will not be able to be done easily in an O-O language, due to size or speed *requirements?* Once you move on to an implementation focus, the language choice can have an effect on the design. For example, some languages support multiple inheritance and some don't.

Make sure the average method size is small. A large average method size (nine lines or more for Smalltalk) is a clear flag that there may be design problems. Function-oriented designs will cause higher average method size numbers.

Also watch out for function-oriented code if using a hybrid O-O language, such as C++, since developers will be tempted to code as they have done before. Again, standard function-oriented constructs, such as *case* statements and lots of *if* statements, are not as common in O-O code and should be viewed as warning signs. An additional problem with hybrid languages is that it is not as apparent when you are dealing with an object and when you're not. In pure languages, such as Smalltalk, there is no question about what you are dealing with, and therefore you must think in terms of objects all the time. This certainly helps to internalize the new paradigm.

Part of the coding effort is documentation, both updates to design documentation and creation of information for help and on-line user documentation. The help and on-line user documentation should be produced iteratively along with the code, initially *by the developers.* Support organization staff should then "clean up" the on-line product documentation *soon after* it is delivered for a build. While this technique has the drawback of wasting effort documenting code that does not make it into the final product, it gains from the same benefits that the iterative testing does, in that the documentation is not built on predictions of deliveries, followed by adaptations in a time crunch when monolithic deliveries are made later in the cycle.

Some of the implementation work could be done by generator-type tools. For example, methods of the proper name that included the description could be taken from the *class cards* and class contracts could be put in a *classComment* method (see Appendix J.3, "Smalltalk Coding Standards").

Design UI classes to exercise the model classes. Work with your usability group and customers to make sure the interface is effective.

UNIT TEST CLASSES: The developers should test their classes before putting them into a build for others to use. The test should be driven by the use case and requirements.

A test case is really a series of messages to send to the (single) class being tested. The developer specifies the message to send, the expected result, and the acceptance criteria (such as *isTypeOf*). Each test step (message) can use the previous step's results, a saved value from an earlier step, or a hard-coded value (this is not shown in the diagram). Control structures, such as conditions and looping, would need to be supported. The mechanism for running the test case can be semi-manual, such as using the Smalltalk debugger and stepping through the execution, or automated, through a *Test Management Facility*. An automated system would obviously help in the effort and should include other features, such as logging of the expected results, actual results, test criteria, and a pass/fail flag.

Tools could also help by coordinating information between the *Change Management* and *Test Management* facilities, indicating which components need to be retested and which have been covered by a test.

FUNCTION TEST CLASSES: As the builds are done during the production period, test cases also iterate and function tests are run. Development should deliver the iteration line item status to the test team along with the driver builds. This can be in various forms, such as a project scheduling tool output. The test team will use this to guide their efforts. They then run tests and feed problem reports back to the development team to resolve. These can take a variety of forms. A set of problem report requirements are contained in Appendix H.2, "Problem Report Requirements."

ASSESS PERFORMANCE, QUALITY, REUSABILITY: The emphasis is on meeting final product assessment criteria. These are inputs to the next iteration's planning period.

4.3.4.10 Iterate until requirements met

Continue to work on subsystem implementations until the requirements are satisfied.

Target Class: BalanceInquiryTransaction

	Message	Expected Result	Acceptance Criteria
1	createFor: aCustomer	aBalanceInquiryTransaction	isTypeOf
2	currentBalance: anAccount	aFloat	isTypeOf
3			
4			
5			

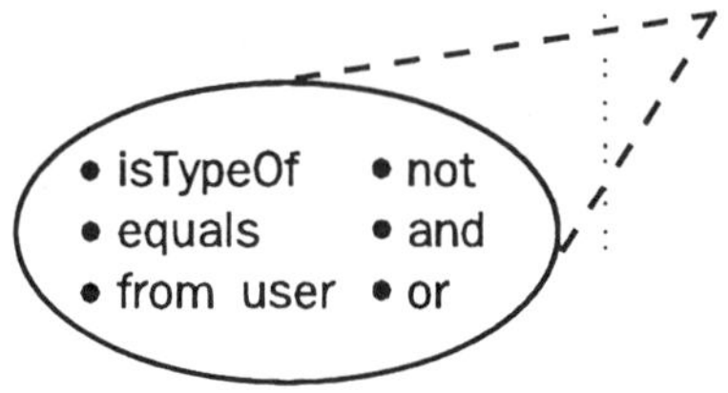

- isTypeOf   • not
- equals   • and
- from user   • or

	Message	Actual Result	Pass/Fail
1	createFor: aCustomer	aBalanceInquiryTransaction	Pass
2	currentBalance: anAccount	anInteger	FAIL
3			
4			
5			

Figure 4.14 Balance Inquiry Test Case

4.3.4.11 Test subsystems

As they are built, the subsystem's contracts can be tested, independently of tests of other subsystems or classes. This black-box testing allows pieces of the system to be finalized separately. The subsystems can be developed in parallel or serially.

4.3.4.12 Document final subsystem designs

The design of the system is important for future changes and should be maintained along with the code. The design information collected as the development progressed should be cleaned up to a final form for this release of the product.

4.3.4.13 Document final architecture

The interface architecture, including external and internal protocols, is a key asset to control and maintain. It is almost directly driven by the requirements, since items such as contracts relate to the basic functional requirements of the system. The architecture should be cleaned up in a final document for this release.

4.3.4.14 Document final user manual

The user's manual information, originally derived from use cases and UI prototyping, must be finalized to deliver with the product. This may be delivered on line or via hard copy.

4.3.4.15 System test the complete system

Once the (sub)system is built, the function tests feed into one complete system test to verify the entire requirements document. You may want to stress test the system, asking beta test users to try to break it. Repeating the same request a large number of times and unusual sequences of actions are examples of ways to make sure the system is truly robust.

4.3.5 Deliverables

The design and test phase has the following deliverables:

1. Quality product code for each subsystem

    This is the code that must meet all product requirements as well as all quality standards for the company. This includes class definitions, including state data, method logic for the classes, and documentation.

    Well-designed O-O methods are very short, on average. The first O-O development effort I was on, staffed by O-O novices, had an average method size of six lines of Smalltalk code. I believe we would have had a lower number if we did better (i.e., more reusable, more truly object-oriented) implementations. Time and again, I have seen code collapse as the abstractions and/or delegations of responsibilities dawned on our team. If you have large method averages, you do not have good O-O designs.

    Most of your time in implementation will be in reading code. This is to look for objects to reuse, either through inheritance or delegation, and to look for code to copy and modify for new uses. My friend Jeff McKenna, whom I consider to be one of the best O-O designers in the world, says he spends 80 percent of his time reading code! There is only so much screen real estate available in browsers. Also, if your methods are short (they should be!), there are typically only three to six lines/method for Smalltalk. C++ lines of code run about three times those for Smalltalk. Do not obscure the code with voluminous comments, in-line archivals of previous code segments, and so on. Comments and archival of code are certainly good things to have around—but not in the methods! First of all, this is not (or at least should not be) function-oriented code (and it certainly is possible to "write C code" in Smalltalk!), so there is not the need for long comment blocks. Changes also tend to be replacements of methods. Since the methods are objects themselves, they can have comments and versions as attributes. In fact, these are support-tool requirements for the process and methodology being proposed.

2. Design documentation

   The documentation will contain as-built deliverables according to the methodology steps outlined in other sections of this book.

ATM DESIGN RELATIONSHIPS

   The *ATM* is the controller of the UI equipment and prompting. It also holds the currentTransaction and can cancel the transaction before it is submitted. The currentTransaction, which is of a particular type (withdrawal, deposit, balanceInquiry, transfer) is created once the customer is identified (this takes place by a collaboration of the *ATM* and the *Bank*, which holds the *Customer* objects). The currentTransaction then requests any further information needed from the ATM.

   The designs for the *account management* and *interface* subsystems of the ATM application are shown in Figure 4.15 and Figure 4.16.

The class responsibilities are derived by walkthroughs of the system functions, assigning responsibilities to the various classes. The ATM class responsibilities and state data derived from walking through use cases and looking at responsibilities and collaborations follow.

ATM CLASS DEFINITION

The following table summarizes the behaviors and state data identified for the ATM object class. Appendix D, "Complete ATM Application," lists behaviors and data for all the classes, along with the rest of the ATM application.

RESPONSIBILITY	DESCRIPTION
account	Get the account object the customer wants to take actions against.
amount	Get the dollar and cent amount the customer wants to use in his or her transactions on the current account.
targetAccount	Get the account object the customer wants to use as the destination of actions.
sourceAccount	Get the account object the customer wants to use as the source of actions.
showAmount: anInteger	Display anInteger amount to the customer on my display.
cancel	Tell my currentTransaction to cancel itself.
transactionLoop	Iterate on customer requests, initiating transactions.

DATA	DESCRIPTION
location	My geographic location.
status	My status. Current status values are: 1. *OK* 2. *Equipment problems* 3. *No money*
currentTransaction	The transaction object that is currently being processed. Only one transaction is allowed to be active at one time for a single ATM machine.

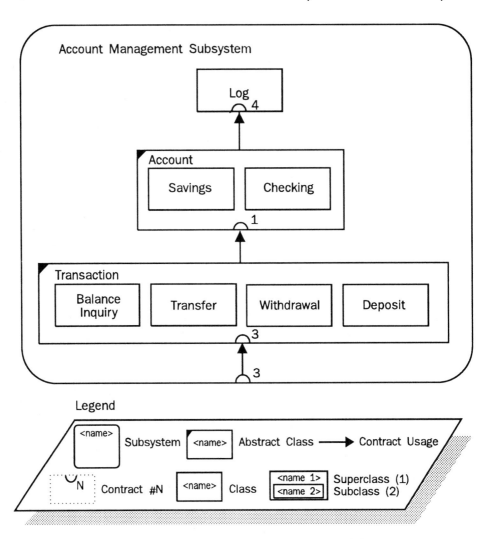

Figure 4.15   ATM Design—Account Management Subsystem

4.4 PACKAGING PHASE

The packaging phase is done once per product development. This is the final phase of product development. During this phase, all the activities necessary for the business to place the product on the marketplace are done. Since each company has its own activities during this phase and most of them do not depend on the process or methodology presented here, I only briefly discuss these activities for closure.

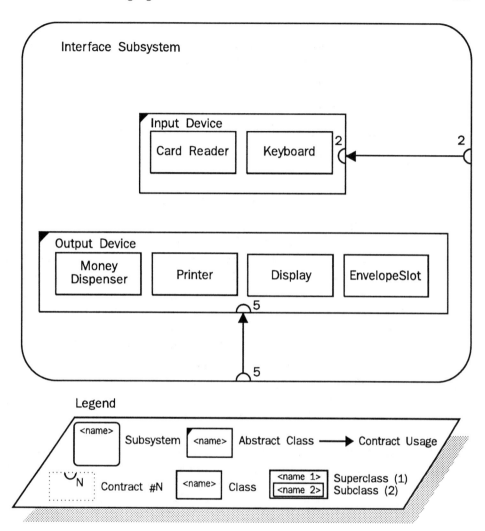

Figure 4.16 ATM Design—Interface Subsystem

4.4.1 Prerequisites

The packaging phase has the following prerequisites:

1. *Quality product code for each subsystem.* This is the key output of the design and test phase. Obviously, without product code there is nothing to package.

2. *System design documentation.* The design information is maintained with the code. The design should be supported by the company tools for software development.

3. *User manual.* This will be key for setting up training.

4.4.2 Activities

The packaging phase has the following activities:

1. Search for reusable components.
2. Translate product.

4.4.2.1 Search for reusable components

The class programmers (Appendix F, "Development Team Roles") are responsible to find new abstractions to expand the reuse library. The packaging phase is the official time to do this (although other times are possible), since the code is now solid. Things to search for include similar classes in different applications, similarities between application and reuse library classes, and classes addressing new areas for the business.

The extra work required to create these reusable components and add them to the reuse library is an investment with payback on future projects in the company. The process must schedule time for this effort, with management's support, for reuse to happen. If you don't contribute to the company's key software asset—the reuse library—you will reach a productivity plateau (see Figure 4.17).[10]

This plateau occurs because the classes that are being reused, which is one of the primary means of higher productivity, are not being added to. So, good abstract classes such as *Collection* are being taken advantage of in new efforts, but new classes *specific to your company's business* are not being created. Granted, they may be created in an ad-hoc way, over and over again on project after project, but this is not the means of leveraging what's been done before. By cleaning up, documenting, testing, certifying, and advertising good, reusable classes, the company's software assets are built up and the next project has more to reuse.

4.4.2.2 Translate product

If the product is to be used by customers that speak different languages, the product may need to be translated into multiple versions.

---

[10]This diagram is from Mark Lorenz, "Getting started with object technology: effectively planning for change," *Hotline on Object-Oriented Technology*, 2, No. 11, (September 1991), pp. 9–12.

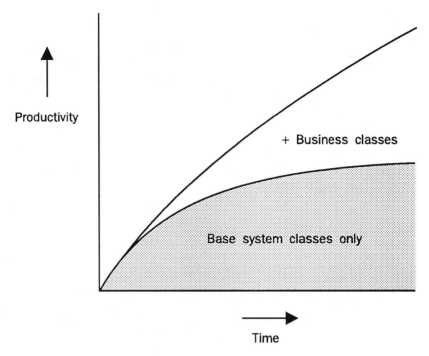

Figure 4.17   Productivity Plateau

4.4.3 Deliverables

The packaging phase has the following deliverables:

1. Final product code
2. New reuse-library components

4.5 SUMMARY

In developing software, we are obviously trying to build what the customer wants in the most profitable manner possible. This means we build the best product on the market in the lowest-cost manner. In order to do this, a four-phase approach is recommended:

---- PHASES ----

1. Business
2. Analysis
3. Design and Test
4. Packaging

By having the design and test phase follow the analysis phase, the focus starts with the *problem domain* and *then* the *solution domain.*

The model and UI are developed as separate, parallel paths because it is important to keep the two relatively independent. The main reason for this is that the model for your business can be reused in many different applications with very little change.

4.5.1 Business Phase

The business phase starts the software development process going. This phase's activities are done once (versus iteratively) before the start of the analysis phase.

4.5.1.1 Activities

The business phase has the following activities:

1. Identify and document types of users.
2. Identify and document initial user requirements.
3. Contact customers interested in a development partnership.

4.5.1.2 Deliverables

The business phase has the following deliverables:

1. *Initial customer requirements document draft.* This document will contain the initial system requirements.
2. *Statement of target customer.* This includes a statement of the type of customer as well as a list of customers willing to participate in the development effort.

4.5.2 Analysis Phase

The analysis phase uses an iterative prototyping technique to develop its deliverables. Even though it is called the analysis phase, it has design and implementation characteristics of the prototype development. The emphasis, however, is on the system analysis and corresponding documentation of a detailed requirements specification and system architecture draft. The feasibility of the project can also be verified during this activity. Scheduling will be largely driven by discussions and evaluations with the customer. The work is exploratory, geared toward flushing out requirements details. The areas to work on during an iteration should be the least understood, highest-risk areas. Once the requirements are well-defined, the project moves on to the design phase.

4.5.2.1 Activities

The analysis-phase activities are summarized in Appendix C, "Methodology Summary," and are not detailed here.

4.5.2.2 Deliverables

The analysis phase has the following deliverables:

1. *Detailed requirements specification.* The requirements specification concentrates on the *functions* needed by the users of the system. The functions are discussed in terms of *what* is to be done, and not *how* it is to be done.

2. *System architecture draft.* This includes a definition of the key classes in the system and the architected interfaces (contracts) for the key classes. It also may include, depending on system size, an identification of subsystems.

3. *User's manual draft.* This is an example of the desired user interface.

4. *Throwaway prototype code.* The prototype facilitates effective communication between the different groups working on the development effort.

4.5.3 Design and Test Phase

The design and test phase uses an iterative development technique to develop subsystem components. This code evolves into the final product code.

4.5.3.1 Test overview

A strategy for testing is to focus your testing on one class at a time in bottom-up fashion. By that, I mean that you want to run a test with only one unverified piece—the class under test.

The developers are responsible to *unit* test their own functional line item code. You should *expect to write as much or more test code as production code.*

The test case is made up of *test steps,* which are themselves comprised of *setup, probe,* and *evaluate* portions. Traditionally testing had a long delay time to verify the "predictions" contained in the specifications. Using the iterative technique, testing closely follows function delivery and itself iterates on test cases.

ITERATIVE TESTING: The goals for using iterative testing are:

1. *To minimize the impacts to test from development changes.* Due to the iterative nature of development using the IDP, changes to test are

going to be fast and frequent. Testing needs to iterate in a similar manner for its activities.

2. *To reduce development cycle time.* Rapid feedback to development throughout the effort allows impacts of errors to be reduced, thereby shortening the overall cycle time.

REUSE LIBRARY TESTING: More extensive "unit" testing of classes (more accurately called *acceptance* testing) occurs when they are "complete." It is at this time that abstractions are again looked for and created, if possible.

4.5.4.1 Activities

Design-phase activities are discussed in Appendix C, "Methodology Summary," and are not detailed here.

4.5.3.3 Deliverables

The design and test phase has the following deliverables:

1. *Quality product code for each subsystem.* This is the code that must meet all product requirements as well as all quality standards for the company.
2. *Design documentation.* The outputs of the methodology presented in this book should be maintained along with the code.

4.5.4 Packaging Phase

The packaging phase is done once per product development. This is the final phase of product development. During this phase, all the activities necessary for the business to place the product on the marketplace are done.

4.5.4.1 Activities

The packaging phase has the following activities:

1. Search for reusable components
2. Translate product

4.5.5 Deliverables

The packaging phase has the following deliverables:

1. Final product code
2. New reuse-library components

Chapter 5

Putting It All Together

*Tradition is what you resort to when you don't have
the time or the money to do it right.*

Kurt Herbert Adler

5.1 PHASES, PROCESS, AND METHODOLOGY

We've talked in detail about the software development phases, the iterative development process, and the object-oriented development methodology. Let's review how they relate to each other. Figure 5.1 pictorially shows the relationships between the phases, process, and methodology.

The *development phases* form the framework for the entire effort. They define the prerequisites and deliverables for different sets of efforts in developing software.

The *iterative development process* (IDP) defines the steps to manage the development efforts. This process is used within the analysis and design phases.

The *object-oriented development methodology* defines the steps in developing quality O-O software. The methodology is used within the production portion of the IDP.

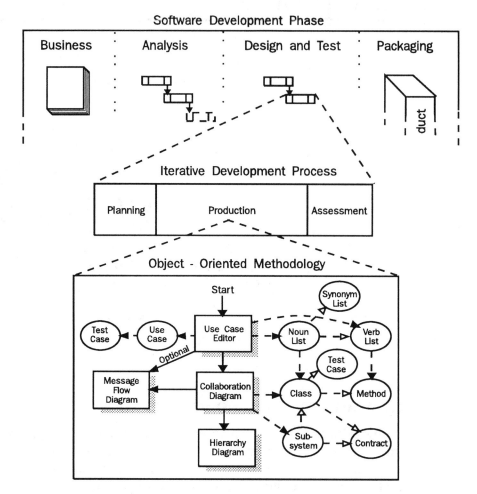

Figure 5.1   Development Phases, Process, and Methodology

5.2 THE DIRTY WORD

Maintenance generally has a bad connotation in the software industry today. If you've noticed, we've not talked much about maintenance. The reason is that maintenance is not viewed as being handled any differently with respect to the topics covered in this book. The iterations that occur on the evolving system during the design phase are really modifications to an existing base, in this case the currently evolving version of the system being developed.

It's true that at the extremes, consisting of both a brand new, large system and a minor "tweak" to an old, monolithic system, maintenance has significantly different meanings.

- A brand new system does not have the maintenance aspects to deal with (although it certainly must interface to other equipment and/or systems), but once design iterations have started, the efforts are *from* a base *to* a new base, which is what the dirty word is all about.

- A minor change to existing code is not really dealt with in this document. If it is truly a minor change, many of the steps detailed here can be skipped. This may also be true of a new function that is almost identical to one already in the system (probably implemented in a subclass). In these cases, the development team must use its discretion to decide what to do and what not to do. Certainly, the design information should be updated for a number of reasons, including minimizing the learning curve. The design takes on new importance if it is used by tools to partially automate the implementation process.

The emphasis in product releases should be on the requirements and architecture. The product implementation should become more and more composed of reuse-library (off-the-shelf) components, as shown in Figure 5.2. It has been estimated that up to 85 percent of all software in existence today could be composed of reusable components and only 15 percent is product specific.[1] Others have given estimates in the 40 percent to 60 percent range. The point is not the exact percent, but rather that we are creating too much code from scratch.

5.3 EXISTING SYSTEM INTEGRATION

Software developed as described in this book can be integrated with existing systems in a variety of manners:

1. Messaging between executables
2. Glass-top coordination
3. Boundary interface classes

5.3.1 Messaging Between Executables

At the simplest level, the O-O system executable, whether packaged as a Dynamic Link Library (DLL) or Executable File (EXE), can

---

[1]T.C. Jones, "Reusability in Programming: A Survey of the State of the Art," *IEEE Transactions on Software Engineering*, SE-10, No. 5 (September 1984), pp. 488–93.

Product Contents

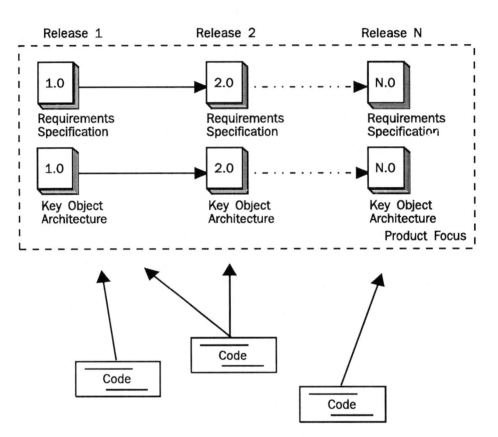

Figure 5.2 Product Component Focus

certainly call non-O-O software and be called by non-O-O software (see Figure 5.3).

In this case, neither side has to know (or care) what the other side consists of, whether objects or functions. The ordering of parameters and collapsing/expanding of objects will happen when going between the two.[2] This black box approach does not integrate the two parts of the system but works around the problem. This is the easiest short-term solution but does not address the remaining long-term incongruities between the system parts.

---

[2]Upon leaving the world of objects, data streams consisting of logical integers, characters, and so on are created ("collapsing" the objects). Upon reentering the world of objects, objects are recreated from information in data streams ("expanding").

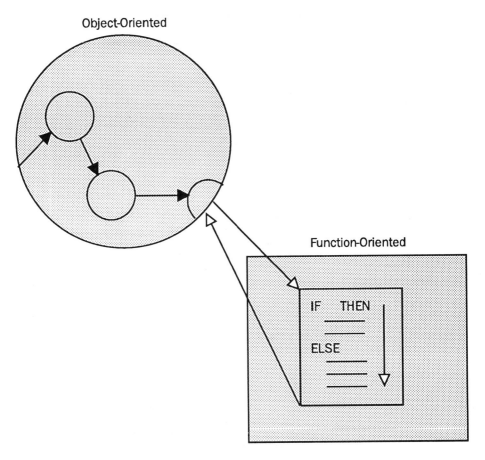

Figure 5.3   Messaging Between Executables

5.3.2 Glass-top Coordination

This type of integration has to do with integrating the old and new code at the user interface (UI) or "glass top" (i.e., the monitor screen). As user interfaces move more and more toward an O-O approach, you will see direct manipulation being used more. This implies actions such as "dragging" and "dropping" objects, in the form of icons, between containers (such as folders), and on top of other objects (such as the trashcan) on the screen. When this occurs, the objects involved must work together to take the appropriate action(s), which can vary greatly. If one of the objects is really function-oriented code, the object-oriented code will probably use an interface object to talk to the functional code (see Figure 5.4).

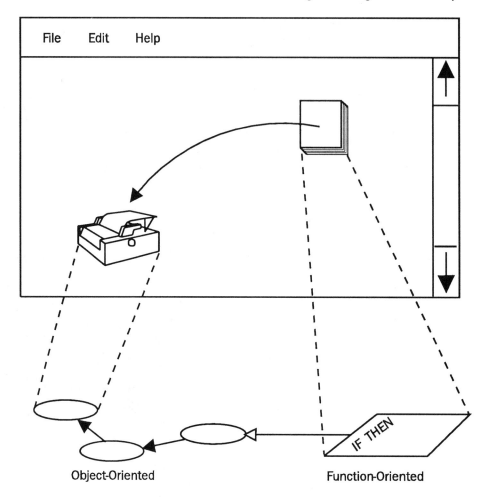

Figure 5.4 Glass-top Coordination

Objects that live on the boundary of the O-O and function-oriented world, providing the interface between the two, are sometimes referred to as *wrapper* objects. They put an O-O "package" around the non-O-O objects, so that the rest of the O-O system does not have to deal with the fact that they are outside that world. In this way, the interface code is localized (encapsulated!) in the few objects that lie on the boundary between the world of objects and the world of functions.

5.3.3 Boundary Interface Classes

Classes are created for objects *outside* the boundaries of the new system, in order to facilitate the O-O portion of the system dealing with the function-oriented code as if it were O-O.

These types of objects are discovered by an analysis that goes "beyond" the domain of functionality that is being created in the O-O portion of the system. This allows the phasing in of new O-O code over time and buffers the other objects from knowing about the function-oriented world around them. Eventually, you must reach the boundary of the O-O world and provide the interface to "flatten" the objects so that the two portions of the system can work together.

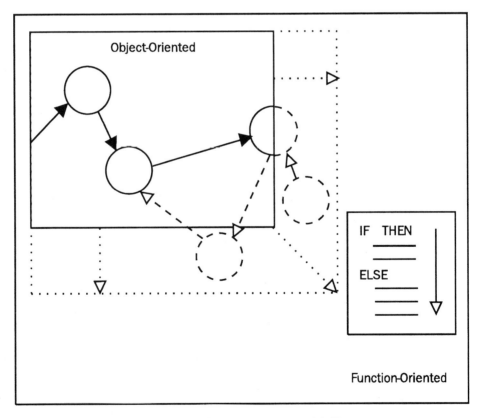

Figure 5.5 Boundary Interface Model Classes

5.3.4 Coexistence

The O-O and function-oriented parts of the system can exist "amicably" together. Certainly, reuse what you can of the existing system, as long as it meets your requirements. Over time, more and more of the function-oriented parts of the system can be replaced by O-O implementations. Certainly, new functions can be written in an O-O fashion, but as maintenance costs of old parts of the system grow, they become candidates for a rewrite. This is also a good opportunity to utilize a new technology like O-O.

You want to make sure to minimize the message traffic between the O-O and function-oriented parts of the system. There is an overhead cost in going between the two—so draw the boundaries between the two at points of low coupling.

5.4 GETTING STARTED

It's always nice to have some advice from those who have gone before about the potholes to avoid and the keys to success. Here is my advice on getting a good start at developing successful O-O systems:[3]

1. Get training. Experienced functional developers are not experienced O-O developers. Remember to get training for *management* too! David Taylor has a good book for your managers to read.[4]

2. Get O-O expertise as a part of your team. At least initially and until you can transfer expertise to your own development team, it is critical that you involve experts at doing good O-O designs and implementation. This will not come from a one-week class. Availability of expertise is critical for success. The expertise can be through on-site consultant(s) and/or off-site apprentice programs. Once you develop some in-house expertise, leverage the experts by having them lead design reviews and acting as "mentors" to new people.

3. Buy or make tools. Tools do not have to be automated to be useful. CRC index cards are useful for O-O analysis. Group development support tools are essential, especially in the areas of change management (configuration control, collecting changes made, filing in changes, and so on) and the build process.

---

[3]These points are adapted from Mark Lorenz, "Getting started with object technology: effectively planning for change" in *Hotline on Object-Oriented Technology*, 2, No. 11 (September 1991), pp. 9–12.

[4]David A. Taylor, PhD., *Object Oriented Technology: A Manager's Guide* (Reading, MA: Addison-Wesley Publishing Co., 1991).

4. Follow a process and methodology. The goal of this book is to give you a possible process and methodology to follow. Whether you use this one or another, use *something!* Some other possible methodologies, as listed in Appendix A, "References," include those by Rebecca Wirfs-Brock, Ivar Jacobson, Bertrand Meyer, and Peter Coad.

5. Set up a reuse library. The company's competitive edge will come from its reuse library. Set up rewards to support reuse.

6. Set up metrics and collect statistics. You're going to have to *prove* that new ways of doing business are beneficial.

7. Use small teams. Break larger problems into multiple small teams. Putting your teams on a LAN is essential, given the speed and volume of changes.

Expect the first project using O-O technology to take *longer!* You have a learning curve and process changes to deal with. The real gains from O-O technology and an iterative process are:

- building the system that meets your needs
- reuse on *future* projects
- lower maintenance costs

5.5 SOME FINAL COMMENTS AND WORDS OF ENCOURAGEMENT

5.5.1 The Comments . . .

The information presented in this book came from a variety of sources, including O-O project experiences, O-O analysis and design books, conferences such as the ACM conference on Object Oriented Programming Systems, Languages, and Applications (OOPSLA) and ObjectWorld, articles from journals such as the *Journal of Object-Oriented Programming (JOOP)*, and discussions with experts in the field such as Jeff McKenna, Reed Phillips, Brad Cox, Peter Coad, Dave Thomas, and Tom Love. I have attempted to provide the best coverage of the key issues related to developing O-O software systems, but must note that O-O development is still in a relatively infant stage. As such, I expect some churn in the industry before solid practices, notations, and processes are standardized.

I would encourage comments, suggestions, and project experiences as inputs to future enhancements to this book. As in other exploratory work (such as software development), I expect to iterate on the content presented here. Your help in making that content the best it can be would be greatly appreciated.

5.5.2 . . . and Words of Encouragement

For those of you that are limping from "bleeding edge" wounds, let me assure you that my project team personally experienced the quantum leaps in productivity that can be achieved with O-O languages and environments. I have seen milestones pulled in by months, thousands of methods developed by a team of six in three months, and snowballing of speed of function delivery as reuse really comes into play.

The level of reuse will peak at the level of the base system you are using (e.g., Smalltalk) if you do not add to this base. Planning for reuse is critical for this to happen—if you do not schedule time and reward people for creating reusable classes, they will not be made. If you add classes to your reuse library (see Appendix F, "Development Team Roles") for your specific industry, you will see a continuing, almost exponential growth in productivity.

The low rate of software systems being built with traditional techniques that meet requirements and are delivered on time and within budget gives us no choice but to try something else. For today, the best "something else" is *objects*.

> In an era when hardware is a commodity and software is the key competitive technology, computer makers that exploit object-oriented software best are likely to dominate the computer industry itself.[5]

Good luck, and be in touch if I can help in any way!

5.6 SUMMARY

The *development phases* form the framework for the entire effort. They define the prerequisites and deliverables for different sets of efforts in developing software. The *iterative development process* (IDP) defines the steps to manage the development efforts. This process is used within the analysis and design phases. The *object-oriented development methodology* defines the steps in developing quality O-O software. The methodology is used within the production portion of the IDP.

Maintenance is not viewed as being handled any differently with respect to the topics covered in this document. Once design iterations have started, the efforts are *from* a base *to* a new base.

---

[5]John W. Verity and Evan I. Schwartz, "Software Made Simple," *Business Week,* (September 30, 1991), p. 94.

The emphasis in product releases should be on the requirements and architecture. The product implementation should become more and more composed of reuse library (off-the-shelf) components.

5.6.1 Existing System Integration

Software developed as described in this book can be integrated with existing systems in a variety of manners:

1. Messaging between executables
2. Glass-top coordination
3. Boundary interface classes

The O-O and function-oriented parts of the system can exist "amicably" together. Over time, more and more of the function-oriented parts of the system can be replaced by O-O implementations. Certainly, new functions can be written in an O-O fashion, but as maintenance costs of old parts of the system grow, they become candidates for a rewrite. This is also a good opportunity to utilize a new technology like O-O.

5.6.2 Getting Started

1. Get training.
2. Get O-O expertise as a part of your team.
3. Buy or make tools.
4. Follow a process and methodology.
5. Set up a reuse library.
6. Set up metrics and collect statistics.
7. Use small teams.

The low rate of software systems being built with traditional techniques that meet requirements and are delivered on time and within budget gives us no choice but to try something else. For today, the best "something else" is *objects*.

Appendix A

References

1. Barnett, Jeff, et al., *Iterative Development Process Guide*, Draft 1, IBM 11000 Regency Parkway, Cary, NC, June 27, 1990.

2. Booch, Grady, *Object-Oriented Design with Applications.* Redwood City, CA: Benjamin/Cummings Publishing Company, 1991.

3. Cheatham, Thomas J., and Lee Mellinger, "Testing object-oriented software systems," *ACM 18th Annual Computer Science Conference Proceedings,* 1990, pp. 161–165.

4. Chidamber, S.R., and C.F. Kemerer, "Towards a metrics suite for object-oriented design," *OOPSLA '91 Conference Proceedings,* (October 1991), pp. 197–211.

5. Coad, Peter, and Ed Yourdan, *Object-Oriented Analysis.* Englewood Cliffs, NJ: Prentice Hall, 1990.

6. Cox, Brad J., *Object-Oriented Programming: An Evolutionary Approach.* Reading, MA: Addison Wesley Publishing Company, 1987.

7. Cunningham, Ward, and Kent Beck, *A Laboratory for Teaching Object-Oriented Thinking SIGPLAN Notices,* vol. 24, (October 1989).

8. Dean, Hal, "Object-oriented design using message flow decomposition," *Journal of Object-Oriented Programming,* (May 1991), pp. 21–31.

9. DeMarco, Tom, *Structured Analysis and System Specification.* Englewood Cliffs, NJ: Prentice Hall, 1979.

10. Gabriel, Richard P., "Solving the Software Crisis," *Unix Review,* 9, no. 7, (July 1991), pp. 27–30.

11. Gause, Donald C., and Gerald M. Weinberg, *Exploring Requirements: Quality Before Design.* New York: Dorset House Publishing Co., Inc., 1989.

12. Gilb, Tom, *Principles of Software Engineering Management.* Reading, MA: Addison Wesley Publishing Co., 1988.

13. Goldberg, Adele, and David Robson, *Smalltalk-80, The Language and Its Implementation.* Reading, MA: Addison Wesley Publishing Co., 1983.

14. Hellanack, Leslie, "IDC's First Object Technology Survey," *First Class,* (September/October 1991), pp. 14–15.

15. Jacobson, Ivar, Object-Oriented Software Engineering: A Use Case Driven Approach. Reading, MA: Addison Wesley Publishing Company, 1992.

16. Jacobson, Ivar, "The Industrial Development of Software Using an Object-Oriented Technique," Objective Systems SF AB, Box 1128, S-164 22, KISTA, Sweden, 1990.

17. Jacobson, Ivar, "Object-Oriented Development in an Industrial Environment," *OOPSLA '87 Conference Proceedings,* Orlando, FL (October 1987), pp. 183–191.

18. Jones, T.C., "Reusability in Programming: A Survey of the State of the Art," *IEEE Transactions on Software Engineering,* SE-10, no. 5 (September 1984), pp. 488–493.

19. Koenig, Andrew, and Bjarne Stroustrup, "Exception Handling for C++," *Journal of Object-Oriented Programming,* (July/August 1990), pp. 16–33.

20. Kolbe, Kathy, *The Conative Connection.* Reading, MA: Addison Wesley Publishing Co., 1990.

21. LaLonde, Wilf R., Jim McGugan, and Dave Thomas, "The Real Advantages of Pure Object-Oriented Systems or Why Object-Oriented Extensions to C are Doomed to Fail," *COMSAC Conference Proceedings, IEEE,* 1989, pp. 344–350.

22. Lorenz, Mark, "Real World Reuse," *Journal of Object-Oriented Programming,* (November/December 1991), pp. 35–39.

23. Lorenz, Mark, "Getting started with object technology: effectively planning for change," *Hotline on Object-Oriented Technology,* 2, no. 11 (September 1991), pp. 9–12.

24. Lorenz, Mark, "Object-Oriented Development: Not Business As Usual," *Hotline on Object-Oriented Technology,* 1, no. 7 (May 1990), 1–4.

25. Lorimer, F. G. et al., *Managing the Development of Object-Oriented Applications,* GG24-3581-00, IBM International Technical Support Center, Boca Raton, FL, 1990.

26. Love, Tom, "Timeless design of information systems," *Object Magazine,* (November/December 1991), pp. 42–48.

27. Meyer, Bertrand, *Object-Oriented Software Construction*. Englewood Cliffs, NJ: Prentice Hall, 1988.

28. Meyer, Bertrand, "The New Culture of Software Development: Reflections on the Practice of Object-Oriented Design," *Technology of Object-Oriented Languages and Systems Proceedings* (TOOLS), 1989, pp. 13–23.

29. Purchase, Jan A., and Russel L. Winder, "Debugging tools for object-oriented programming," *Journal of Object-Oriented Programming*, (June 1991), pp. 10–27.

30. Rettig, Marc, "Testing Made Palatable," *Communications of the ACM*, 34, no. 5 (May 1991), pp. 25–29.

31. Rumbaugh, James, et al., *Object-Oriented Modeling and Design*. Englewood Cliffs, NJ: Prentice Hall, 1991.

32. Sakkinen, M., "Disciplined Inheritance," *Proceedings of the 1989 European Conference on Object-Oriented Programming* (ECOOP), pp. 39–56.

33. Sankar, Chetan S., "The Role of User Interface Professionals in Large Software Projects," *IEEE Transactions on Professional Communication*, 34, no. 2 (June 1991), 94–99.

34. Shlaer, Sally, and Stephen J. Mellor, *Object Lifecycles: Modeling the World in States*. Englewood Cliffs, NJ: Yourdon Press, 1988.

35. Soley, Richard, "Combined ORB Submission Completed," *First Class*, (September/October 1991), p. 5.

36. Stroustrup, Bjarne, *The C++ Programming Language*, Reading, MA: Addison Wesley Publishing Company, 1987.

37. Taylor, David A., PhD., *Object-Oriented Technology: A Manager's Guide*. Reading, MA: Addison-Wesley Publishing Co., 1991.

38. Tracz, Will, *Software Reuse: Emerging Technology*. Los Alamitas, CA: IEEE Computer Society Press, 1989.

39. Verity, John W., and Evan I. Schwartz, "Software Made Simple," *Business Week*, September 30, 1991, pp. 92–100.

40. Wild, Frederic H., III, "Managing Class Coupling," *Unix Review*, 9, no. 10 (October 1991), pp. 45–47.

41. Wirfs-Brock, Rebecca et al., *Designing Object-Oriented Software*. Englewood Cliffs, NJ: Prentice Hall, 1990.

Appendix B

Tool References

This list of tools is not comprehensive. It is meant to indicate some of the tools that are available that could be used to support the process and methodology in this book.

Note: The tools listed here are for informational purposes only. Listing a tool does *not* imply any endorsement.

B.1 METHODOLOGY TOOLS

1. ObjectMaker

   Mark V Systems (818) 995-7671. ObjectMaker is an O-O analysis and design tool that supports multiple methodologies and notations, including Rumbaugh, Coad, and Booch.

2. ObjectOry

   Objective Systems 46 8 703 45 30 (Sweden). ObjectOry is a tool to support Ivar Jacobson's ObjectOry methodology. The methodology leads a developer from requirements through design, including use cases and message flows. Implementation is not covered.

3. OOATool

   Object International, Inc. (512) 795-0202. OOATool is a PC-based diagramming tool that supports Peter Coad's O-O analysis notation for collaboration diagrams. It runs on Smalltalk/V Mac and V PM.

4. OOSA

   Hewlett-Packard Company (408) 746-5955. OOSA supports an O-O systems analysis, including noun list extraction from documents and state transition diagrams.

5. Pilot

   Semaphore Tools, Inc. (508) 686-9850. Pilot is an O-O analysis and design tool that supports Semaphore's notation for C++ development.

6. Rational Rose

   Rational (408) 496-3700. Rose supports an O-O analysis and design using Booch's methodology and notation. It runs on the Sun SPARC and IBM RISC System/6000 workstations under Motif and OpenWindows GUIs.

B.2 IMPLEMENTATION TOOLS

1. AM/ST

   Coopers & Lybrand SoftPert Systems Division (617) 621-3670. AM/ST supports LAN-based group development under Smalltalk/V PM.

2. Application Organizer Plus

   Instantiations, Inc. (800) 888-6892. Application Organizer Plus supports group development for Objectworks/Smalltalk users.

3. C++

   AT&T Unix Systems Labs, Inc. (201) 644-3884. C++ supports O-O programming with extensions to the C language. C++ compilers are available from a number of companies, including Borland and Zortech.

4. GemStone

   Servio Corporation (800) 243-9369. GemStone is an Object DBMS.

5. Geode *Servio Corp.* (800) 243-9369. Geode is a development environment built on top of Servio's GemStone database.

6. Eiffel

    Interactive Software Engineering (805) 685-1006. Eiffel is a language and support tool. It includes integrity structures such as assertions and runs on Apple, IBM, HP, and other workstations.

7. ENFIN/2

    ENFIN Software Corporation (619) 549-6798. ENFIN/2 provides an O-O development environment similar to Smalltalk.

8. Envy

    Object Technology International (OTI) (613) 228-3535 (Canada). Envy is a multideveloper support tool for Smalltalk/V286, V PM, and V Mac systems. It includes versioning, including methods, class ownership, and more. It is *not* a database management system.

9. NexpertObject

    Neuron Data (415) 321-4488. NexpertObject is a rule-based, O-O development system that runs under DOS, OS/2, and Unix.

10. Objective-C

    The Stepstone Corporation (203) 426-1875. Objective-C supports O-O programming.

11. Objectkit

    ParcPlace Systems (415) 691-6700. Objectkit contains classes to enhance the base hierarchy. It has versions that run on Sun, HP, IBM, DEC, and Apple workstations.

12. ObjectCraft

    ObjectCraft, Inc. (415) 540-4889. ObjectCraft allows C++ developers to visually program their applications.

13. Objectworks/Smalltalk

    ParcPlace Systems (415) 691-6700. Objectworks/Smalltalk supports O-O programming. It has versions that run on Sun, HP, IBM, DEC, and Apple workstations.

14. Parts

    Digitalk (213) 645-1082. Parts is capable of laying out UI objects and connecting them to non-UI (model) objects to develop an application window under Smalltalk/V.

15. Profiler/V

    First Class Software (408) 338-4649. Profiler/V is a performance profiler for Smalltalk/V Windows and/V PM.

16. Prograph

    TGS Systems (902) 429-5642. Prograph allows programmers to develop logic visually.

17. Smalltalk/V

Digitalk (213) 645-1082. Smalltalk/V supports O-O programming including browsers, debugger, and numerous classes. It has versions that run under DOS, OS/2, Windows, and the MacIntosh.

18. Smalltalk-80

ParcPlace Systems (415) 691-6700. Smalltalk-80 supports O-O programming, including browsers, debugger, and numerous classes. It has versions that run on a variety of platforms.

19. Tigre Programming Environment

Tigre Object Systems, Inc. (408) 427-4900. Tigre is a tool to develop graphical user interfaces for applications running under Objectworks/Smalltalk.

20. Versant

Versant Object Technology Corporation (415) 325-2300. Versant is an Object DBMS. The tools that come with the DBMS include a screen layout, class modeling, query interface, and report writer. Versant supports C, C++, Smalltalk-80, and Smalltalk/V PM.

21. WindowBuilder/V

Acumen Software (415) 649-0601. WindowBuilder/V allows you to create your application's UI interactively under Smalltalk/V Windows and /V PM.

Appendix C

Methodology Summary

C.1 ANALYSIS PHASE

1. Write use cases.

   Write down what you heard the users say the system should do in descriptive text scenarios.

2. Verify use cases with customers.

   Go over the new system scenarios with the users, making any changes necessary.

3. Extract and document requirements from use cases.

   Pull out the underlying requirements from the scenarios. These are the functional and informational needs of *what* the system is to provide, and not *how* the system is to provide it.

4. Extract nouns from use cases.

   Look for salient nouns in the text. Think about implied objects when the passive voice is used.

   a. Associate verbs from use cases with nouns.

      Look for verb phrases that are used with nouns.

5. Identify and document application classes from the noun list.

Go over the noun list, identifying classes for those nouns that are important to the application being built. Throw out extraneous nouns. Describe the newly identified classes. Maintain traceability to the requirements derived from the use case.

a. Identify and document responsibilities from the verb list.

Go over the verb list for a new class and document related method names and descriptions. Maintain traceability to the requirements derived from the use case.

6. Walk through use cases, using the identified application classes.

The analysts step through the use cases, discussing what classes would do what in order to provide the required functions.

a. Draw message flow diagrams (optional).

Document the message flows between the classes in order to provide the required functions.

b. Expand responsibilities as needed.

Document additional or modified responsibilities for the classes that are discovered as a part of the use-case walkthrough.

c. Add new classes as needed.

Document additional classes that are discovered as a part of the use-case walkthrough.

7. Prototype use cases.

In the prototyping language, model the current understanding of the system for one or more use cases.

8. Verify prototype with customer.

Show the prototype to the users, discussing what functions and information are provided.

a. Functionality.

Verify the required functionality.

b. User interface.

Usability must verify the user interface requirements (if any) that specifically apply to the application, such as certain information being provided together or other information being accessible from certain types of fields being presented. Avoid making too many UI requirements, which will lock too much of the "how" of the design in too early and result in change management problems.

9. Update use cases and requirements as needed.

The requirements document is *the* key deliverable of the analysis phase and must be maintained. The use cases are inputs to the test team for test cases and to information development for the user's manual, and therefore should be updated.

10. Iterate steps 7 through 9 for areas that don't have solid requirements.

    This is essentially the IDP iterations that are used to firm up the requirements. The iterations don't spend much time on scheduling, with most of the effort on prototyping (production) and assessment.

C.2 DESIGN AND TEST PHASE

1. Review the analysis-phase deliverables.

    Make sure the design team understands the requirements. Review the analysis prototype (*demonstration* not implementation). Review the UI requirements.
    a. Validate the architecture draft.

        Review the draft architecture (classes, responsibilities, and any subsystems that were defined).
    b. Expand responsibilities as needed.

        Document additional or modified responsibilities for the classes that are discovered as a part of the design walkthrough.
    c. Add new classes as needed.

        The *analysis* phase identified the key classes in the problem domain. Document additional classes that are discovered as a part of the design walkthrough. In particular, pay attention to implementation-specific areas, such as device-related and target-platform classes.

2. Document the target language, hardware, and software platforms.

    These will be decided implicitly or explicitly by the requirements.

3. Search the reuse library for applicable off-the-shelf components.

    The focus is now on building the real system. There may be solid components in the company's reuse library, which is stocked by previous projects' classes, applications, and tools.

4. Look for overlap of responsibilities, similarity of types of objects.

    Overlap of responsibilities and similar object types indicate a missing abstract class and/or subclassing possibilities.
    a. Create application mini-hierarchies.

        Application abstract classes and subclass relationships in general form hierarchies within some of the classes in the application. These hierarchies (and the other classes) will have to be optimally placed in the overall class inheritance hierarchy.

5. Draw collaboration diagrams.
   a. Identify and document subsystems.

   Break the system into functionally cohesive black boxes that can be developed relatively independently. This may be done in the analysis phase for large systems, in order to manage the complexity.
   b. Identify and document contracts.

   Look at the key responsibilities of classes and subsystems.

6. Draw message flow diagrams.
7. Walk through the design diagrams and documentation.

   Ask questions such as: "Do these objects have enough information and collaborations with other objects to do their work?" "Execute" some message flows to make sure that the design makes sense.

   You should also be concerned with implementation-specific questions, such as: "Do I need a backward pointer from this object?" You must make trade-offs—back off from "pure" O-O designs as the pragmatics (such as performance) require.

   As Object Database Management Systems (ODBMS) come into wider use, you will want to plan for clustering of objects to and from the disk and cache. Most systems today already offer this capability, with default clustering provided. Performance tuning will almost certainly require "tweaking" the way the persistent object cache works.
   a. Expand responsibilities as needed.

   Document additional or modified responsibilities for the classes that are discovered as a part of the design walkthrough.
   b. Add new classes as needed.

   Document additional classes that are discovered as a part of the design walkthrough. In particular, pay attention to implementation-specific areas, such as device-related and target-platform classes.

8. Implement subsystems.

   The subsystems are connected via the defined contracts only. Subsystems can be treated as black boxes from other subsystems. The implementation of different subsystems can run in parallel or serially and uses the IDP.

a. Look for abstractions.

These will greatly help with the implementation and are prime candidates for the reuse library. Abstract classes will help reduce your code volume and the related maintenance load.

b. Write methods.

Code the methods in the target language. An O-O language will map better from the O-O design. Make sure methods are small, on average. Watch out for function-oriented code if using a hybrid O-O language, such as C++.

c. Unit test classes.

The developers should test their classes before putting them into a build for others to use. The test should be driven by use cases and requirements.

d. Test performs function tests on classes.

As the builds are done during the production period, test cases also iterate and function tests are done.

e. Assess performance, quality, reusability.

The emphasis is on meeting final product assessment criteria.

9. Iterate subsystem development until requirements are met.

10. System test the complete system.

Once the (sub)system is built, the function tests feed into one complete system test to verify the entire requirements document.

Appendix D

Complete ATM Application

The methodology analysis and design objects for the ATM application are presented together here. Normally, there would be UI application classes, such as windows and panes. This appendix focuses on the application model objects. The ATM application does not have a complex UI. Any UI classes included would not be central to the design—these same model classes could be used with different UIs.

D.1 ATM USE CASES

Note: Key words in the ATM use cases are shown in *italics*. These words relate to possible classes or class responsibilities.

─────────── **ATM APPLICATION USE CASES** ───────────

1. ATM access failure
2. Balance inquiry
3. Cash deposit

4. Cash withdrawal
  a. $200 maximum withdrawal per day (variation)
  b. default and specified withdrawal amount (variation)
5. Account fund transfer

ATM USE CASE—FUNCTION ACCESS (REUSED FOR OTHER USE CASES)

A machine is available outside the *bank* for *customers* to perform typical *teller* functions. *Customers* have *cards* that have a unique *identification* and *password* that they insert into a slot in a *card reader*. The *customer* is prompted for the *password* that is enscribed on the *card*. If the two match, the *customer* is given a menu choice of actions on the *screen*.

If the two do not match for *three* times in a row, the *card* is kept by the *card reader* and the *customer* is shown a *message* on the screen.

ATM USE CASE—BALANCE INQUIRY

<Function Access Use Case prerequisite> If the *balance inquiry button* is pressed, the *customer* is asked for the *account* type, after which a *receipt* is *printed* which contains the *account name* and *number,* date, and amount of money in the *account*. The *customer* is allowed to then request another action, or to exit.

ATM USE CASE—CASH DEPOSIT

<Function Access Use Case prerequisite> If the *deposit button* is pressed, the *customer* is asked for the *account* type and an *amount* of money to be *deposited*. The *envelope slot* then opens, and the *customer* puts the *envelope* into it. A *receipt* is then *printed* which contains the *account name* and *number,* date, and amount of money *deposited* to the *account*. The *customer* is allowed to then request another action, or to exit.

**ATM USE CASE—
CASH WITHDRAWAL**

<Function Access Use Case prerequisite> If the *withdrawal button* is pressed, the *customer* is asked for the *account* type and an *amount* of money to be *withdrawn*. The *money dispenser* then dispenses the requested amount of money. A *receipt* is then *printed* which contains the *account name* and *number,* date, and amount of money *withdrawn* from the *account*. The *customer* is allowed to then request another action, or to exit.

<Variation—$200 maximum withdrawal per day> If the *withdrawal* for a particular *account* would put the daily *amount* over the $200 limit for the day, a *receipt* is immediately *printed* with a *message* explaining why no money can be *dispensed*.

<Variation—Default withdrawal amount> If the *customer* picks the *default button,* then $30 is immediately *dispensed,* without asking for an amount.

**ATM USE CASE—
ACCOUNT FUND TRANSFER**

<Function Access Use Case prerequisite> If the *transfer button* is pressed, the *customer* is asked for the source *account* type and the target *account* type and an *amount* of money to be *transferred*. A *receipt* is then *printed* which contains the *account names* and *numbers,* date, and amount of money *transferred* between *accounts*. The *customer* is allowed to then request another action, or to exit.

D.2 ATM Collaboration Diagrams

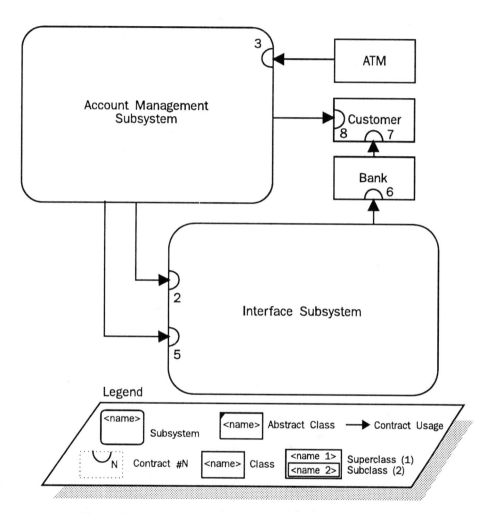

Figure D.1 ATM Collaboration Diagram—ATM Application

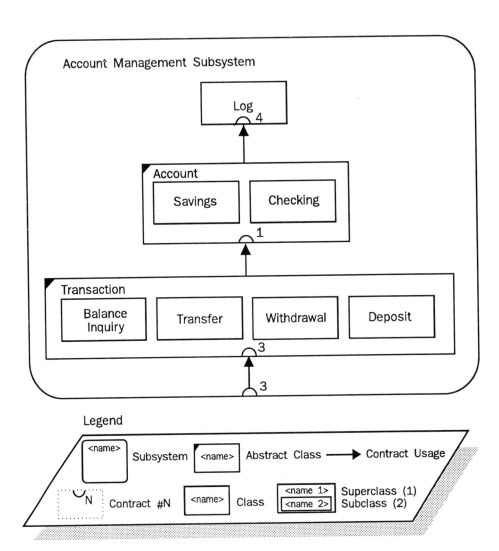

Figure D.2   ATM Collaboration Diagram—Account Management
Subsystem

ATM Application Design

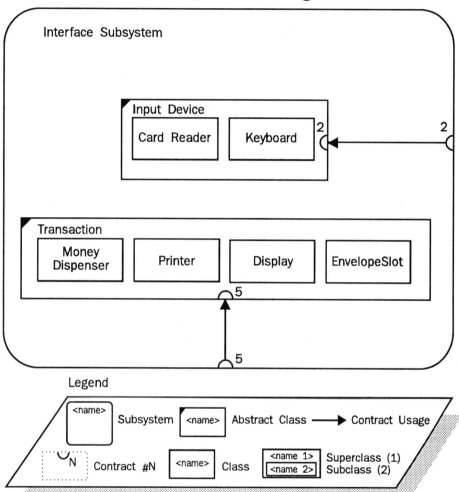

Legend

Figure D.3 ATM Collaboration Diagram—Interface Subsystem

D.3 ATM SUBSYSTEMS

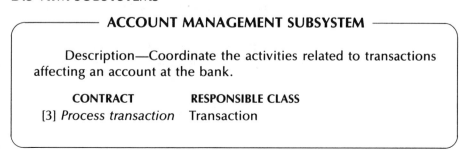

──────── ACCOUNT MANAGEMENT SUBSYSTEM ────────

Description—Coordinate the activities related to transactions affecting an account at the bank.

CONTRACT   **RESPONSIBLE CLASS**
[3] *Process transaction* Transaction

INTERFACE SUBSYSTEM

Description—Coordinate the devices used by the ATM machine to transfer information to and from the bank's customers.

CONTRACT	RESPONSIBLE CLASS
[2] *Get user input*	InputDevice
[5] *Put output to the user*	OutputDevice

D.4 ATM CONTRACTS

CONTRACT 1— MAINTAIN ACCOUNT BALANCES

Description—Provide basic account balance functions, such as deposits, withdrawals, and inquiries.
Server—*Account*
Clients—*Transaction, TransferTransaction, Withdrawal Transaction, DepositTransaction, BalanceInquiryTransaction*

CONTRACT 2—GET USER INPUT

Description—Handle inputs from the ATM user, including keyboard and card.
Server—*InputDevice*
Clients—*ATM*

CONTRACT 3—PROCESS TRANSACTION

Description—Process the customer account services available at the ATM machine, including transfers, deposits, withdrawals, and inquiries.
Server—*Transaction*
Clients—*ATM*

CONTRACT 4—LOG TRANSACTIONS

Description—Save transaction information for audit purposes.
Server—*TransactionLog*
Clients—*Transaction*

CONTRACT 5—
PUT OUTPUT TO THE USER

Description—Handle outputs to the ATM customer, including money, receipts, and display messages.
Server—*OutputDevice*
Clients—*Transaction*

CONTRACT 6—VERIFY TRANSACTION

Description—Make sure that a transaction can be started for the customer, including verifying the access password.
Server—*Bank*
Clients—*InputDevice*

CONTRACT 7—VERIFY ACCOUNT

Description—Make sure that this customer has an account with the access password.
Server—*Customer*
Clients—*Bank*

CONTRACT 8—VERIFY WITHDRAWAL

Description—Make sure that a withdrawal will not cause the daily limit to be exceeded.
Server—*Customer*
Clients—*WithdrawalTransaction, CheckingAccount*

D.5 ATM HIERARCHY DIAGRAMS

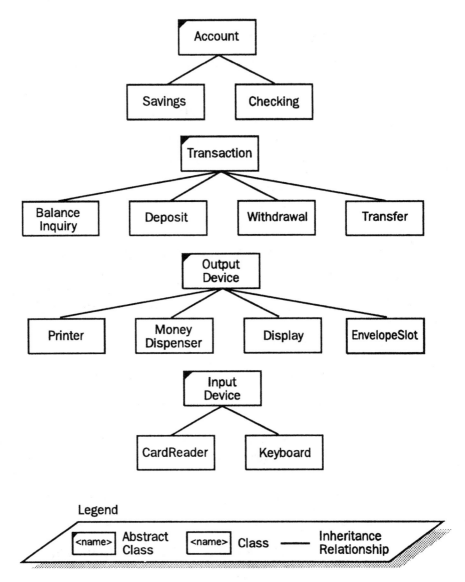

Figure D.4   ATM Application Inheritance Hierarchies

Note: Classes not shown do not have hierarchical (inheritance) relationships with other ATM *application* classes.

D.6 ATM CLASS DEFINITIONS

The following table summarizes the behaviors and state data identified for the ATM object classes.

ACCOUNT CLASS

Description—The *Account* class is an abstract class that provides common services for all types of bank accounts.
Superclasses—*PersistentObject*
Subclasses—*SavingsAccount, CheckingAccount*

CONTRACTS

1. [1] **Maintain account balances** is implemented by the following public method(s):
   a. withdraw:
   b. deposit:
   c. balance

RESPONSIBILITY	DESCRIPTION
balance	Return my current balance.
balance: anAmount	(Private) Set my current balance to anAmount.
deposit: anAmount	Add anAmount to my current balance.
withdraw: anAmount	Subtract anAmount from my current balance.

DATA	DESCRIPTION
balance	The amount of funds I currently hold.
withdrawalLimit	The amount of funds that can currently be withdrawn from me.

ATM CLASS

Description—The *ATM* class is the class responsible for providing the teller machine services for bank customers, creating the appropriate *Transactions*. There is one instance of this class for each ATM machine.
Superclasses—*Object*
Subclasses—None
Contracts—None

RESPONSIBILITY	DESCRIPTION
account	Get the account object the customer wants to take actions against.

amount	Get the dollar and cent amount the customer wants to use in his or her transactions on the current account.
targetAccount	Get the account object the customer wants to use as the **destination** of actions.
sourceAccount	Get the account object the customer wants to use as the **source** of actions.
showAmount: anInteger	Display anInteger amount to the customer on my display.
cancel	Tell my currentTransaction to cancel itself.
transactionLoop	Iterate on customer requests, initiating transactions.
DATA	**DESCRIPTION**
location	My geographic location.
status	My status. Current status values are: 1. *Down* 2. *No money*
currentTransaction	The transaction object that is currently being processed. Only one transaction is allowed to be active at one time for a single ATM machine.

BALANCEINQUIRYTRANSACTION CLASS

Description—The *BalanceInquiryTransaction* class services account balance inquiry requests. These (and all) transactions are created by the *ATM* class. These (and all) transactions are transient, ceasing to exist after the request is serviced.

Superclasses—*Transaction*
Subclasses—None

CONTRACTS

1. [3] **Process transaction** is implemented by the following public method(s):
   a. balance:

RESPONSIBILITY	**DESCRIPTION**
balance: anAccount	Tell the customer anAccount's current balance.

BANK CLASS

Description—The *Bank* class manages the overall bank, including keeping track of customers and accounts. There is one and only one instance of this class.

Superclasses—*PersistentObject*
Subclasses—None.

CONTRACTS

1. [6] **Verify transaction** is implemented by the following public method(s):
   a. validateCustomerNumber:
   b. validatePassword:

RESPONSIBILITY	**DESCRIPTION**
validateCustomerNumber: anInteger	
	Compare anInteger to my customers. Return true if it is a customer of mine, false if it is not.
validatePassword: aPassword forCustomer: aCustomer	
	Compare aPassword to the aCustomer's password. Return true if it is equal, false if it is not.
maximumWithdrawalPerDay: anAmount	
	(Private) Set the maximum amount of cash that can be withdrawn in any one day from a single account to anAmount.
DATA	**DESCRIPTION**
customers	My current customer list.
atmMachines	My current list of ATM machines.

BUSINESSRULE CLASS

Description—The *BusinessRule* class enforces the bank's business rules during the execution of an application, by monitoring object state values (through accessing methods).
Superclasses—*PersistentObject*
Subclasses—None.
Contracts—None.

CARD CLASS

Description—The *Card* class emulates the customers' ATM access cards, verifying the password and identifying the user. There is one instance of this class for each ATM customer.
Superclasses—*PersistentObject*
Subclasses—None.
Contracts—None.

RESPONSIBILITY	DESCRIPTION
number	Return my account number.
DATA	**DESCRIPTION**
numbers	My owner's account number(s).

CARDREADER CLASS

Description—The *CardReader* class handles the reading of the users' ATM access cards. There is one instance of this class for each of the bank's ATM machines.
Superclasses—*InputDevice*
Subclasses—None.

CONTRACTS

1. [2] **Get user input** is implemented by the following public method(s):
   a. card

RESPONSIBILITY	DESCRIPTION
card	Wait for a customer to insert a card.

———— CHECKINGACCOUNT CLASS ————

Description—The *CheckingAccount* class manages a customer's checking account, providing check processing and other specialized services. The general account management functions are inherited from *Account*.

Superclasses—*Account*
Subclasses—None.

CONTRACTS

1. [1] **Maintain account balances** is implemented by the following public method(s):
   a. withdraw:

RESPONSIBILITY	DESCRIPTION
withdraw: anAmount	Subtract anAmount from my current balance. Create a loan at the prevailing rate if current balance < 0.

———— CUSTOMER CLASS ————

Description—The *Customer class* is a sort of data repository, maintaining information about the bank's customers. There is one instance of this class for each customer.

Superclasses—*PersistentObject*
Subclasses—None.

CONTRACTS

1. [7] **Verify account** is implemented by the following public method(s):
   a. validatePassword:

2. [8] **Verify withdrawal** is implemented by the following public method(s):
   a. withdrawalLimitReached:

RESPONSIBILITY	DESCRIPTION
withdrawalLimitReached: anAmount	Answer true if anAmount + currentAtmWithdrawals > the maximum allowed for one day.
validPassword: aPassword	Answer whether aPassword equals my current password.

name	Return my name.
address	Return my address.

DATA	DESCRIPTION
password	My current password.
accounts	My current accounts.
name	My name.
address	My address.
currentAtmWithdrawals	The amount of money I have withdrawn from ATM machines today.
id	My unique ID.

DEPOSITTRANSACTION CLASS

Description—The *DepositTransaction* class services account deposit requests. These (and all) transactions are created by the *ATM* class. These (and all) transactions are transient, ceasing to exist after the request is serviced.

Superclasses—*Transaction*
Subclasses—None.

CONTRACTS

1. [3] **Process transaction** is implemented by the following public method(s):
   a. depositTo:

RESPONSIBILITY	DESCRIPTION
depositTo: anAccount	Credit funds to anAccount. Ask the customer for an amount.

DISPLAY CLASS

Description—The *Display* class handles the presentation of prompts and messages to the customer on the ATM screen. There is one instance of this class for each ATM machine.

Superclasses—*OutputDevice*
Subclasses—None.

CONTRACTS

1. [5] **Output result to user** is implemented by the following public method(s):
   a. displayMessage: aMessage

RESPONSIBILITY	DESCRIPTION
displayMessage: aMessage	Put a message on the ATM display for the user to read.

ENVELOPESLOT CLASS

Description—The *EnvelopeSlot* class manages the opening and closing of the deposit slot on the ATM machines. There is one instance of this class for each ATM machine.
   Superclasses—*OutputDevice*
   Subclasses—None.

CONTRACTS

1. [5] **Output result to user** is implemented by the following public method(s):
   a. openSlot
   b. closeSlot

RESPONSIBILITY	DESCRIPTION
openSlot	Open the slot for envelope deposits.
closeSlot	Close the slot for envelope deposits.

INPUTDEVICE CLASS

Description—The *InputDevice* class is an abstract class to provide common services of all input devices.
   Superclasses—*Object*
   Subclasses—*CardReader, Keyboard*

CONTRACTS

1. [2] **Get user input** is a subclass responsibility.

KEYBOARD CLASS

Description—The *Keyboard* class handles function keys and typewriter-keyed inputs from the user. There is one instance of this class for each ATM machine.
Superclasses—*InputDevice*
Subclasses—None.

CONTRACTS

1. [2] **Get user input** is implemented by the following public method(s):
   a. character

RESPONSIBILITY	DESCRIPTION
character	Wait for a customer to press a key on the ATM keyboard. Return the value.

MONEYDISPENSER CLASS

Description—The *MoneyDispenser* class manages the dispersal of cash to the user via the money slot. There is one instance of this class for each ATM machine.
Superclasses—*OutputDevice*
Subclasses—None.

CONTRACTS

1. [5] **Output result to user** is implemented by the following public method(s):
   a. dispense:

RESPONSIBILITY	DESCRIPTION
dispense: anAmount	Give the user anAmount of money, which must be in $5 increments.

OUTPUTDEVICE CLASS

Description—The *OutputDevice* class is an abstract class to provide common services of all output devices.
Superclasses—*Object*
Subclasses—*Printer, MoneyDispenser, Display, EnvelopeSlot*

CONTRACTS

1. [5] **Output result to user** is a subclass responsibility.

PRINTER CLASS

Description—The *Printer* class manages the hard-copy outputting of transaction receipts. There is one instance of this class for each ATM machine.
Superclasses—*OutputDevice*
Subclasses—None.

CONTRACTS

1. [5] **Output result to user** is implemented by the following public method(s):
   a. printReceipt:

RESPONSIBILITY	DESCRIPTION
printReceipt: aTransaction	Print a receipt showing the details of aTransaction, including date, location, transaction ID, account number, and amount.

SAVINGSACCOUNT CLASS

Description—The *SavingsAccount* class manages a customer's savings account, providing specialized services. The general account management functions are inherited from *Account*.
Superclasses—*Account*
Subclasses—None.

CONTRACTS

1. [1] **Maintain account balances** is implemented by the following public method(s):
   a. creditInterest

RESPONSIBILITY	DESCRIPTION
creditInterest	Add the interest for the last month to my current balance.

TRANSACTION CLASS

Description—The *Transaction* class is an abstract class to provide common services to all transactions.
Superclasses—*Object*
Subclasses—*BalanceInquiry, Deposit, Withdrawal, Transfer*

CONTRACTS

1. [3] **Process transaction** is a subclass responsibility.

RESPONSIBILITY	DESCRIPTION
amount	Return the amount of money associated with myself.
amount: anInteger	(Private) Set the amount of money associated with myself to anInteger.
account	Return the account associated with myself.
account: anAccount	(Private) Set the account associated with myself to anAccount.
cancel	Rollback any actions taken as part of the current transaction, resetting the state to its status before the transaction began.

DATA	DESCRIPTION
amount	The amount of money associated with myself.
account	The account associated with myself.

TRANSACTIONLOG CLASS

Description—The *TransactionLog* class provides a repository for an audit trail of all transactions at the bank. There is one and only one instance of this class.
Superclasses—*Object*
Subclasses—None.

CONTRACTS

1. [4] **Log transactions** is implemented by the following public method(s):
   a. log:

RESPONSIBILITY	DESCRIPTION
log: aTransaction	Put aTransaction's information into a persistent log file.

TRANSFERTRANSACTION CLASS

Description—The *TransferTransaction* class services account-to-account fund transfers. These (and all) transactions are created by the ATM class. These (and all) transactions are transient, ceasing to exist after the request is serviced.
Superclasses—*Transaction*
Subclasses—None.

CONTRACTS

1. [3] **Process transaction** is implemented by the following public method(s):
   a. transfer: from: to:

RESPONSIBILITY	DESCRIPTION
transfer anAmount from: sourceAccount to: targetAccount	Move anAmount of money from the source to the target account.
DATA	**DESCRIPTION**
accounts	The source and target accounts for the transfer action.

WITHDRAWALTRANSACTION CLASS

Description—The *WithdrawalTransaction* class handles fund withdrawals from accounts. These (and all) transactions are created by the *ATM* class. These (and all) transactions are transient, ceasing to exist after the request is serviced.
Superclasses—*Transaction*
Subclasses—None.

CONTRACTS

1. [3] **Process transactions** is implemented by the following public method(s):
a. withdraw: from:
b. withdrawFrom:

RESPONSIBILITY	**DESCRIPTION**
withdraw: anAmount from: anAccount	
	Debit anAmount from anAccount, giving the funds to the customer.
withdrawFrom: anAccount	
	Debit funds from anAccount. Ask the customer for an amount.

Appendix E

Requirements Specification Outline

Remember that you want the requirements specification to be *what is required of the system*, not how it is to be accomplished. Keep the design out! Since requirements are functions the user needs to accomplish some goal or solve some problem, the requirements are stated as end-user functions. These functions are product capabilities that solve user problems—they are not implementation algorithms.

Talking about *functions* may seem incongruous with an O-O development effort, but it is not. Users want an ATM machine to give them money from their accounts at 2 AM . . . they don't care if the software is made out of objects. *But*. . . they do care about understanding what is being delivered and getting the services they desire as quickly as possible. That is where objects step in.

The end-user functional requirements are the key to your system acceptance testing. Other tests, such as class testing, are geared toward developing building blocks that together will deliver the contracted functions.

1. General

   a. Purpose of the Requirements Specification

       State that the document is to:

     1) Serve as the statement of requirements to be satisfied by the system, for mutual understanding between the developers and the customers.

     2) Serve as the basis for system testing.

   b. Terms and Abbreviations

       Define any terms and abbreviations used in the document.

2. System Summary

   a. Background

       Provide any relevant background information about the system being developed, such as what it is replacing and the original motivation for the system.

   b. Objectives

     1) Purpose of the System

       State the high-level objectives of the system.

     2) Composition of the Requirements Specification

       Delineate the functional areas of the system, if they can be grouped into subsystems.

     3) Anticipated Changes

       State any known changes in requirements.

   c. System Definition

       Give an overview of the hardware environment, including systems that interface to the system to be built.

     1) \<name> Subsystem

       For each subsystem, give an overview of the functional requirements.

   d. System Diagrams

       Heading only.

     1) Major System Software Functions

       Show a further breakdown of the functional requirements by subsystem.

     2) Major System Software Functional Relationships

       State any required system-to-system or subsystem-to-subsystem protocols.

     a) \<type> Scenario

       Describe any user scenarios (use cases) that are known to help with initial understanding of the required functionality.

e. Interface Definition

List the interfaces to be supported. They are described in the following sections.

1) <subsystem> to <external system>

Describe the internal equipment interface functional requirements.

f. Assumptions and Constraints

State any assumptions and constraints that are known, including requirement priorities.

3. Detailed Characteristics and Requirements

Heading only.

a. Specific Performance Requirements

Heading only.

1) Accuracy and Validity

State any requirements that relate to accuracy of calculations, and validity of fields received from outside the system to be built.

2) Timing

Very clearly state any timing requirements for display generation and transaction processing. This is often a sticky area—be painstakingly explicit in your statements here.

b. Computer Program Detailed Functional Requirements

Introductory paragraph.

1) <name> Subsystem

For each subsystem, state the detailed requirements. Make sure the format is such that *every individual requirement* is easily referenced and separate. This is the heart of the requirements document—to be filled in during the analysis phase.

c. Failure Contingencies

Address backup, fallback, and restart requirements.

d. Design Requirements

Discuss coding standards, delivery vehicles (such as files produced by tools), and documentation content.

e. Human Performance Requirements

Talk about usability and interface standards, such as CUA.

4. Environment

Heading only.

a. Equipment Environment

Talk about the target hardware platform.

b. Support Software Environment

Talk about the target software platform.

c. Interfaces

Document details of internal and external protocol formats, such as a communications or report format standard, to be used in the system.

d. Security and Privacy

State any access and/or privacy requirements.

5. Quality Assurance

Give an overview of how the testing is to be done.

a. Unit Tests

Talk about how unit tests are to be done, including by whom and with what tools.

b. Integration Tests

Talk about how integration (function) tests are to be done, including by whom and with what tools.

c. System Test

Talk about how system tests are to be done, including by whom and with what tools.

6. Appendix A—UI Requirements

State any user interface requirements, such as a standard screen layout.

Appendix F

Development Team Roles

The roles in an O-O development effort are different than traditional roles. This is primarily due to two factors: the *iterative development process*, and the emphasis and importance of the *reuse library*. The types of activities that the people are doing in an O-O analysis and design are certainly different too, but the methodology does not affect the team roles as dramatically as the preceding items.

The roles for other groups in the organization are different too. It is important for groups such as test and information development (product publications) to adapt to the iterative development style, working in close coordination with the development process. See "Object-Oriented Development: Not Business As Usual," *Hotline on Object-Oriented Technology*, 1, no. 7 (May 1990), pp. 1–4 by Mark Lorenz for an in-depth look at the organizational implications and suggestions for how to adapt.

The roles shown in Figure F.1 have been successful in past O-O development efforts.[1] The team members are not set in concrete. It is

---

[1]The descriptions of the roles shown here are from project experiences and also discussions with Adele Goldberg of ParcPlace Systems at OOPSLA '90 in Ottawa.

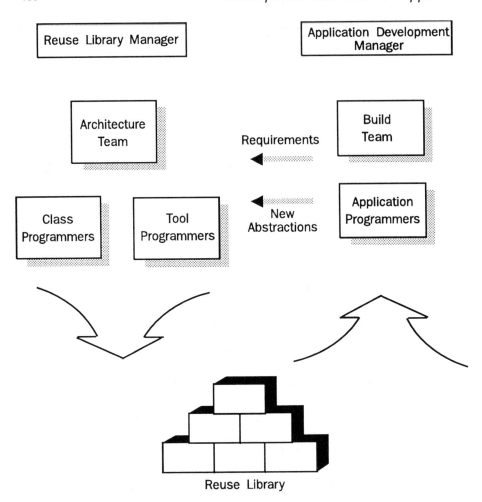

Figure F.1   O-O Development Team Roles

possible to have movement between teams and possibly even to have people included in more than one team at a particular time. The general idea is that these people play roles with specific responsibilities, as described later.

1. Reuse Library Manager

   This is a key role. This person manages the company's key software asset: the reusable classes geared toward the company's industry. The class and tool programmers work for this person.

2. Architect

These people know the company the best. They know the object classes that are important to the company and how they interface to other classes within the reuse library and to systems outside the reuse library. They are responsible for maintaining the interface integrity (i.e., the contracts).

The architects also receive requirements from the application programmers for new services from the reuse library. These may be designed by the architects or passed on to the appropriate class or tool programmer, depending on the type of request. Tools supporting library searches should keep track of successful *and* nonsuccessful requests. *Both* provide important information about the reuse library: the first on existing components being reused; the second on *needed* components.

3. Class Programmer

These are the best O-O designers. They have the most experience at looking for abstractions. They have the broadest view of the company's applications. They own some number of reusable classes. The class programmers' customers are the application programmers.

Obviously any class can be reused by others. The difference is these classes are meant to be reused. They have been through extensive testing and are categorized in the reuse library. Tools to support searches should make it as easy as possible to find the "right" components. This implies that searches can be on user-defined keywords and keyword expressions. Automatic help in categorizing new classes and methods can suggest possible keywords, based on words in object descriptions.

Reusing classes that are not in the reuse library is risky, since the code is probably under current development and has not been thoroughly tested. The classes in the reuse library are typically more general purpose, too. They may be set up as *framework* classes, to be specialized by the application programmers.

The classes come from applications that have used similar, specialized versions of the abstract, general-purpose class. The class programmer is responsible to look for these abstractions within the company's applications to add to the reuse library. This usually happens during the packaging phase of development (Section 4.4, "Packaging Phase"), although it can happen late in the design and test phase (Section 4.3, "Design and Test Phase").

It is also possible for class programmers to participate in the early stages of an application development cycle. This participation is to facilitate *reuse* of components in the company's reuse library. The class programmers can bring expertise in one or more areas, such as communications or UI, along with detailed knowledge of existing classes that relate to these areas. In this way, they can help the new project get a quick start in those areas. An added (and important) benefit is that the reusable components get "polished," becoming more reusable and widely applicable as they are used under different circumstances. This is how the most powerful classes in Smalltalk, such as *Collection*, came about—over time as used by "roving experts." Jeff McKenna recently told me about how Smalltalk developers used to subclass the *Collection* class on a regular basis. Over the years, as it became more elegant in its implementation, developers stopped doing this and reused it through delegation. This process required the classes to *be used* in different situations, with the class owners molding them into better "works of art."

4. Tool Programmer

These programmers are similar in background to the class programmers, but are responsible for developing tools to support O-O development efforts. The makeup of this team can certainly overlap with the class programmers.

The tools should support the development process and methodology described in this document, as well as any other productivity aid to any developer.

5. Application Development Manager

This is the person responsible to build a particular product (or release of a product). The application programmers and build team work for him.

6. Application Programmer

These programmers make up the teams developing applications. The application programmers live in the world of the problem domain. They are *clients* of the class and tool programmers. The types of efforts being done move through the development phases described in Chapter 3, "O-O Development Methodology," so that the programmers in this role are creating an analysis prototype and designing product code at different times in the cycle.

7. Build Team

   This team accepts changes from the application programmers and integrates the changes into a common set of software.
   The build cycle (Appendix G, "Build Cycle,") depends on the organization's needs, but follows standard procedures.

The overall concept is that the architects, class, and tool groups maintain the company's most valuable software asset: the reuse library.
This library is the foundation for ongoing and future application development efforts, by the application and build groups. New requirements and abstractions come from these *clients* of the library.

F.1 WHO SHOULD FILL THESE ROLES

In working with your people, you will come to realize who is good at
creating abstractions, who is good at finding the objects, who is good
at getting the code implemented, and who is good at testing. I'll pass
on one bit of advise from the writings of Kathy Kolbe.[2] She categorizes
people at different levels in four innate ways of performing tasks:

1. Fact finder
2. Follow through
3. Quick start
4. Implementor

Her studies have shown that everyone has some of all of these innate
strengths. The levels in each of them determine the tasks you will resist and have stress dealing with, versus those you will enjoy (you can
still excel in both cases).

   The idea is that you need a mixture of people who are strong in
all of the categories and you need to assign them appropriately. For
example, I am strongest in *fact finder* and *quick start*, with an overall
category of "manager." I am most comfortable in a technical lead
position, where I can scope out what should be done and then dele-
gate the details to others. I can perform in other roles, but I will not be
as comfortable. You may consider looking at your people's strengths
and working toward a mix. I know that companies' cultures tend to
foster similar types of people, and I know of at least one O-O company
that focuses specifically on keeping the right mix and assigning them
appropriately.

---

[2]Kathy Kolbe, *The Conative Connection*, (Reading, MA: Addison Wesley Publishing Co. Inc., 1990), pp. 6–7.

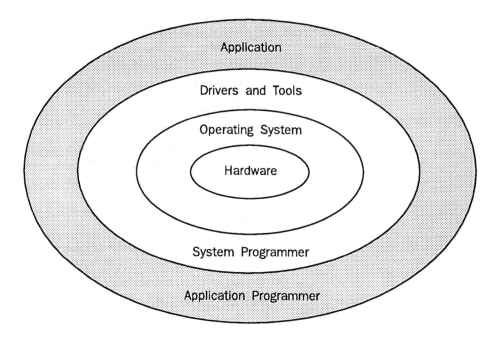

Figure F.2   Function-Oriented View of Applications

F.2 APPLICATION PERSPECTIVE

The perspective that we view applications is different in traditional, function-oriented systems compared to O-O systems.[3] This also provides another slant on the team roles.

In the function-oriented system, the operating system surrounds access to the hardware (see Figure F.2).

Systems programmers build and maintain equipment drivers and basic tools on top of the operating system kernel. The applications sit on top of all this, as an additional layer, built and maintained by applications programmers.

In an O-O system, the application is at the center of the focus (see Figure F.3).

---

[3]The diagrams presented in this section are adapted from a pitch originally delivered by Jeff McKenna of The McKenna Consulting Group.

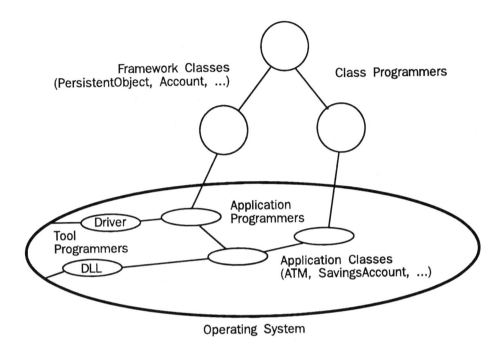

Figure F.3   Object-Oriented View of Applications

The application classes are positioned to inherit from the appropriate framework classes, which provide windowing, graphics, persistence, and other capabilities. The framework classes are built and maintained by the class programmers, who view the application programmers as their clients. Classes that interface to the operating system, such as equipment drivers, are built and maintained by tool programmers.

F.3 TRANSITION STAGES

As team members make the transition to O-O, they move through a number of stages. There are a number of ways to check on how a member is doing. One telltale sign is simply by listening to design discussions—if the person talks about *application* objects, such as tellers, that is a good sign; if the person talks about *computer* objects, such as stacks, then he or she has fallen back on old ways. It takes a while to internalize the new paradigm and it will happen in direct proportion to the amount of time spent in direct contact with people who think *objectively.*

During our project development efforts, the team members transitioned through various stages of expertise. It is worthwhile to discuss the metamorphosis your people will undergo. The following stages were apparent:[4]

1. Novice

    Novices spend their time trying to get their function-oriented heads turned around, so they can see the application object classes. They have a hard time finding the classes and write a lot of function-oriented code. Novices need to have journeymen or gurus around to help them overcome their learning hurdles. The novice stage typically lasts about three to six months.

2. Apprentice

    Apprentices begin to understand what object-orientation really means. They still prefer to work with others, who help foster an environment of discovery. Apprentices begin turning out good designs, although not consistently. Gurus and journeymen still need to keep an eye on apprentices. This period lasts another three to six months.

3. Journeyman

    Journeymen have internalized the O-O paradigm and work independently. They can provide key inputs during design reviews. They still have mental roadblocks that may require a guru to break through. This period can vary greatly in length, but probably will last at least a year.

4. Guru

    Seasoned journeymen work well and independently and are distinguished from gurus only by the speed and inventiveness of their work. For gurus, O-O development comes naturally. A guru automatically sees things in an O-O perspective (and in fact may have trouble seeing them in any other way!), moving quickly through the phases of development during rapid iterations. A guru can move the project over mental hurdles, causing others to see something clearly that eluded them before. This stage lasts

---

[4]This discussion is adapted from Mark Lorenz, "Getting started with object technology: effectively planning for change" *Hotline on Object-Oriented Technology,* 2, no. 11, (September 1991), pp. 9–12.

the rest of your life, if you're good enough to make it.

By my standards, there are very few gurus in the world today. The rest of us will have to rely more on the evolution of proven processes and methodologies to perform effectively and survive our project development efforts.

These stages were pretty clear for us over the years. You can tailor the advice in this book according to the category of people you have on your project. One thing that's for sure—once you go down an O-O path, you won't want to go back. I've yet to see someone successfully make it past the novice stage and even consider thinking about software in other than O-O terms.

Appendix G

Build Cycle

The IDP defines the major project iterations. Within these iterations, there are minor iterations. These minor iterations will be referred to as *build cycles*.

The "grass-roots" strength of iterative development springs from the basic day-to-day development activities. In a traditional approach, the activities are concentrated on a particular phase of activity, such as requirements definition, high-level design, or coding. In iterative development, the day-to-day activities are mini-cycles, moving **rapidly** between phases (see Figure G.1). These phases will be called *activities*, to differentiate them from the analysis and design and test phases focused on in this book. A typical build cycle is twice a week.

G.1 DEVELOPMENT PHASE PATTERNS

During development, the rapid movement between types of activities for any one line item is somewhat predictable. Figure G.2 and Figure G.3 are typical patterns that you can expect to see during the analysis

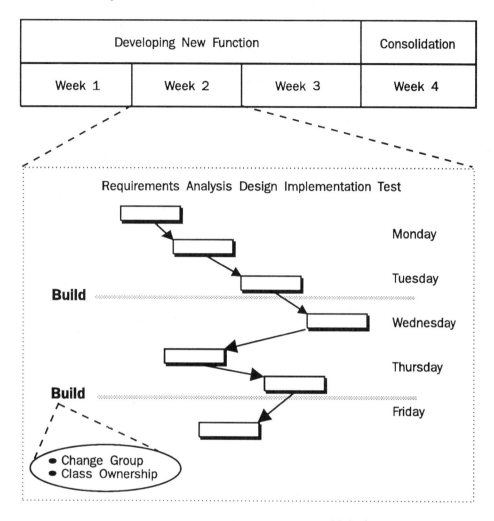

Figure G.1   Iterative Development Build Cycle

and design and test phases, respectively. The differences relate to the emphasis and state of the system during the different phases.

During the analysis phase, there are returns to the requirements, to validate them with users. There is not a lot of effort spent on testing.

During the design phase, there should not be much time spent on requirements. However, a lot of time is now spent on testing.

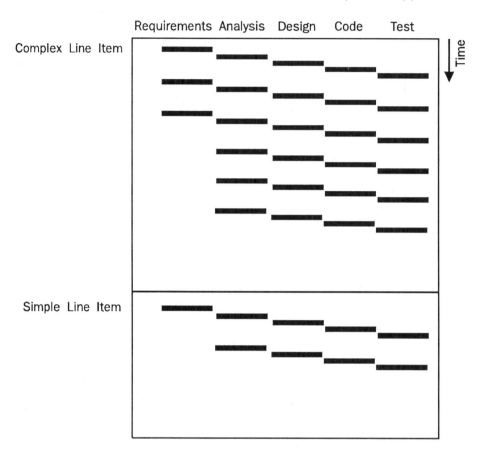

Figure G.2 Typical Analysis Phase Development Patterns

What you should notice is that development activities that have been previously resolved during completed iterations are not repeated. For example, you should not see much *requirements* activities occurring during the design phase. The requirements should have been well defined through the analysis phase iterations. Also, once the design has iterated enough to meet the requirements (e.g., performance), you should not see much return to design activities (if you do, you probably have a case of "feature creep," where an enthusiastic developer wants to keep enhancing a pet class).

Another trend which is not evident from the diagram is that subsequent iterations for the same line item tend to be shorter. So, if the

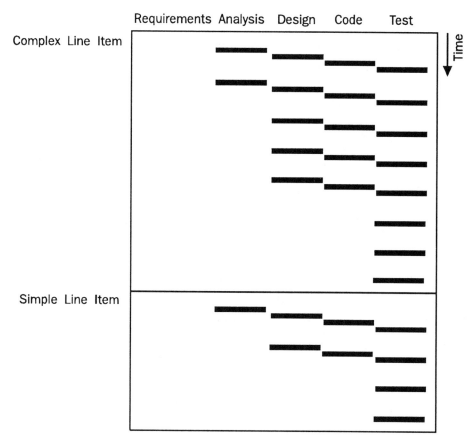

Figure G.3 Typical Design Phase Development Patterns

first iteration on a line item is for five days, the next iteration might be three days, and the final iteration might be one day. During this time, the effort might be cycling between design, code, and test rapidly during the day(s).

G.2 CODING FOCUS

The developer's focus during development shifts from one of adding function, or *application focus*, to consolidation, or *class focus*, and back again (see Figure G.4). This cycle continues throughout the production phase of the IDP. The build cycle is used during both.

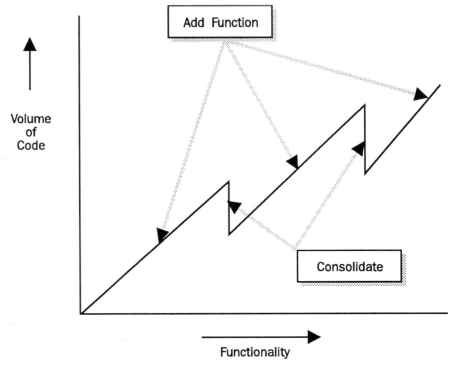

Figure G.4   Coding Focus—Consolidation

The application-focus periods are used for a period of time, such as three weeks (as a rule of thumb). This is when the line items are worked on and functional capabilities are being added.

This period of time is followed by a *consolidation* period, where the class owner's code is cleaned up, more intensive testing is performed, and design reviews are held. During the consolidation period, the developer is focusing on the class design and application architecture, making sure the code is usable, documented, and clean. It is sort of a mini-assessment period, as discussed for the IDP. The consolidation is an *internal* effort only, though. During consolidation, you would expect the volume of code to decrease, as redundant or poorly designed code is cleaned up. The consolidation focus may last for one week as a rule of thumb, but it could vary in length. The consolidation period would normally be shorter than the development period.

G.3 THE BUILD PROCESS

The actual process steps that we have used successfully in the past follow. This process was used for Smalltalk development, but most of the steps could be used for any target language.

1. Collect change groups, containing all modifications to code (or related objects, such as documentation).
    a. Name the application change groups IIIMMYY, where:
        *   III = the developer's initials
        *   MMYY = the target build date
    b. Name change groups for the base system IIIMMYYB, where:
        *   III = the developer's initials
        *   MMYY = the target build date
        *   B = base system changes

    Tools should provide for automatic collection and manipulation of change groups.

2. Add leading actions to the change groups, as needed. These are steps to prepare the system for the changes contained in the change group. For example, the actions may create a new pool dictionary or global that is used in the new code.

    Some leading actions can be collected automatically by the change management tools, such as class and method deletions.

3. Distribute the changes to the appropriate class owners. Use separate files for each set of changes that belong to different owners. Again, tools can automate this step.
    a. Name the distribution change group files IIIMMYY.OOO, where:
        *   III = the developer's initials
        *   MMYY = the target build date
        *   OOO = the class owner's initials

4. Place the resulting distribution change groups into a *pending* directory on the LAN server machine. It is up to the individual developers to check the pending directory for change groups with their initials before the build submittal deadline, so that they have time to examine and incorporate any changes from other developers.

5. Browse the changes sent to you in the *pending* directory. Work with the originating developer, if necessary, to modify the changes. The modifications may be due to better use of the class design or duplication of function.

6. Merge the accepted changes from other developers into your official change group (for your owned classes only). Tools should automate this process.

7. Remove the merged change groups sent to you from the *pending* directory. The person doing the system build can look in the *pending* directory to see what files have not been processed.

8. Edit the *order.doc* file on the server, if necessary, to note any interchange group dependencies for the build. The dependencies have to do with changes that are needed for your changes to file in correctly. The build person uses this file as inputs for the build to set the processing order for the change groups.

9. File out your final change groups for the upcoming build to the server's *changes* directory.

10. Start a new change group for the next build date.

11. Once the build is complete, as notified by the build person, copy the updated system files to your development directory. A batch tool (*getBuild*) can retrieve the files for you.

The build person should archive the system files and should keep copies in another building.

G.4 PROJECT MANAGEMENT TIPS

The following items list suggestions for your development efforts:

1. Use class ownership.

    Class ownership is an integral part of the development effort. Class ownership means that one person on the development team (or in the class programmer group for reuse-library components) *owns* a particular set of classes. The primary reason for using class ownership is that it leads to higher-quality designs and code, since the people take pride in what is "theirs" and are held responsible to fix any problems with their classes. This alleviates the problems typically incurred when someone "rambles through" a set of classes while resolving a problem report or developing new functions.

Tools can capitalize on the use of class ownership, by providing functions such as change distribution to the appropriate person.

2. Establish projects and applications.

Grouping classes according to applications versus according to the inheritance hierarchy, for example, helps people become more productive by focusing attention on the *application* (problem domain) and not the *implementation* (solution domain). It also facilitates submittal of changes on an application basis, which makes more logical sense to people.

Note: Ultimately, all official changes to a class should be passed by the class owner.

3. Establish coding standards.

It is especially important to remember that *reading* code is much more important in a reuse environment (see Appendix J.2, "Common Coding Standards").

4. Establish documentation standards.

Set up standard formats for project documents, including design documentation, with examples. This is important for reuse, both within the project and outside. Documentation standards will be *required* for the reuse library to accept candidate components.

5. Emphasize reuse.

Establish a reuse library (*this will become critical to your company's survival in the software business!*) and reward people for contributing to it and using it to reduce their development cycle. Remember, reuse-library components do not have to be recreated *or* extensively tested—you win *twice!*

6. Have design reviews.

Leverage your best O-O designers to work with your novices. Good functional designs and good O-O designs are not the same! Take time to clean things up and don't be afraid to throw things away (the pieces are small and easily replaced).

7. Establish communication channels.

This is always important. The difference with the type of development described here is that the speed of changes makes easy information dissemination and access critical. Set up some common access mechanism, such as on a server system, that everyone has easy access to. This could be the basic structure for discussion forums to a problem reporting/tracking system.

Appendix H

Sample Line Item Schedule and Description

Many of the scheduling activities are essentially the same as for any development effort. This section deals with the *differences.*

Figure H.1 shows scheduling inputs used as a part of a development plan. These line items would be laid out and tracked using typical Gantt charts, based on dependencies, durations, and resources.

> **Note:** The dependencies with an "E" at the beginning are references to entries in the component's external dependencies table. The items with just a number are references to the same component's item numbers.

A key difference in this scheduling input is that the line items can have multiple (usually up to four) iterations planned for a particular item. The idea is to plan to develop multiple versions of system functions, right from the start. The iterations shown would usually occur in sequential major iterations of the IDP. In other words, all the first iterations of line items related to one functional area would be scheduled during a major iteration driver schedule, so that "version 1" of the functions are available to get feedback from users. The next major IDP iteration would then contain all the second line item iterations, so

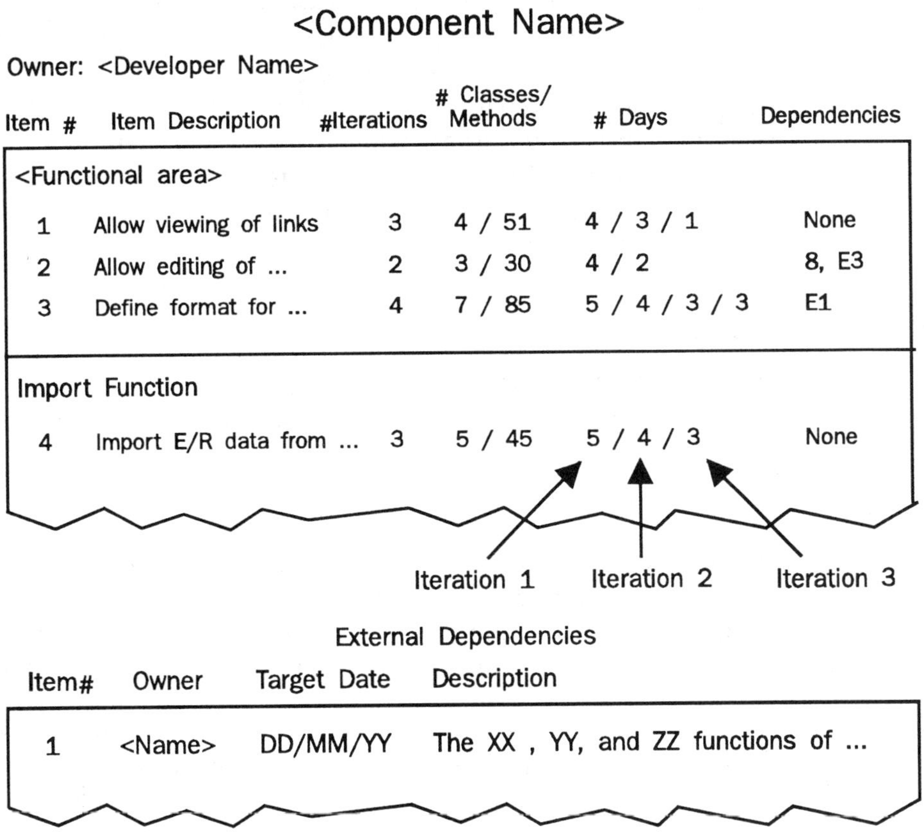

\<Component Name\>

Owner: \<Developer Name\>

Item #	Item Description	#Iterations	# Classes/ Methods	# Days	Dependencies
\<Functional area\>					
1	Allow viewing of links	3	4 / 51	4 / 3 / 1	None
2	Allow editing of ...	2	3 / 30	4 / 2	8, E3
3	Define format for ...	4	7 / 85	5 / 4 / 3 / 3	E1
Import Function					
4	Import E/R data from ...	3	5 / 45	5 / 4 / 3	None

Iteration 1   Iteration 2   Iteration 3

External Dependencies

Item#	Owner	Target Date	Description
1	\<Name\>	DD/MM/YY	The XX , YY, and ZZ functions of ...

Figure H.1   Line Item Scheduling Inputs

that "version 2" of the functions are available. And so on. In this way, users are *effectively* involved all along and unknowns in the system are explored early in the cycle with *plans* for changes as the developers learn more.

The duration of a line item typically would decrease for subsequent iterations, since more is known about the item and more code to support the functionality will exist from the previous iteration(s). For example, Figure H.1 shows line items with decreasing numbers of days for the iterations.

All or some subset of the product functions can be worked on during a single major iteration, depending on the size of the product and the size of the staff. The idea is to set high-level goals for major iterations and have complete versions of product functions delivered in each iteration.

Note that the overall project should plan on some percent of reuse to provide the functions of the product being built. The project should also plan for a percent of functionality contributed to the company's reuse library. These would not directly show up in the line item schedules, but would affect what *becomes* a line item—*and* what work is needed on the line item. There is more work to create a reusable component than a nonreusable one. Will Tracz has estimated that it takes 60 percent more time:[1]

- 25 percent for generalization
- 15 percent for documentation
- 10 percent for testing
- 5 percent for reuse library submission and maintenance

H.1 ESTIMATING

Where did the numbers in the line item inputs shown in Appendix H, "Sample Line Item Schedule and Description" come from? They were estimated by the developer responsible for that line item. What did the developer use to decide on the numbers? Let's talk about that a bit . . . .

Most of the time, a developer "eyeballs" a piece of work and guesses at the amount of effort there. Some typically estimate high and some are habitually optimistic, estimating low. If the developer has done something similar before, then he or she will have some real basis for the estimate, even though it is not very rigorous.

A way to increase the accuracy of your estimates is to base them on something other than "seat of the pants." I would recommend using your company's statistical database of actual experiences with previous projects to create a standard *unit of effort*. This unit would be based on a well-understood class development effort, with examples of other types of classes and their actual efforts.

You don't *have* a company statistical database? Then *start* one! Keep statistics on the number of iterations for classes, the types of classes, the iteration lengths, the number of methods per class, and the method sizes. (See Appendix I. "Measurements and Metrics") Over a subsequent *large* project, you will be able to come close in your estimates of your company's expected productivity rates. The next project (maybe even *yours*) will benefit from it.

---

[1]As discussed by Will Tracz in the IBM SWREUSE on-line forum on 11/6/91.

The following table lists the types of assignments for the amount of effort to develop a class.[2]

ESTIMATING CLASS DEVELOPMENT EFFORT

EFFORT VALUE	DESCRIPTION
1	Class already exists.
3	Similar class exists, needs some extensions via subclass.
5	Similar class exists, needs many changes.
7	New class, but problem is understood.
10	New class, problems are not understood.

Note: These numbers are an example only and should be adjusted to match your company's actual experiences with previous projects.

Once these *effort values* have meaning for your company, you can estimate based on this metric. In the short term, use results of one major iteration to help with better estimating for the *next* iteration. In other words, start using your statistical database now.

H.1.1 Priming Your Company Database

As in any effort, your best estimates are based on past projects. In lieu of those data, there *are* some good design rules of thumb and other companies' experiences available.

Note: There are incongruities between the following sections. I am including both, since they are two data points and this is not an exact science. Use your own judgment to decide what is best for your effort.

H.1.1.1 Rules of Thumb

Based on my group's experiences over the last few years, the following rules of thumb should help you with your estimates (and help identify good O-O designs). These rules are from Smalltalk development— C++ will result in higher line of code (LOC) and statement averages. See Appendix I, Measurements and Metrics, for a complete discussion of these and other guidelines.

1. The average method size should be less than eight LOC. Bigger averages indicate O-O design problems (i.e., function-oriented coding in Smalltalk).

---

[2]The table is adapted from F. G. Lorimer et al., *Managing the Development of Object-Oriented Applications*, GG24-3581-00, Boca Raton, FL: IBM International Technical Support Center, (November 1990), p. 29.

2. The average method size should be less than five statements. Bigger averages indicate O-O design problems.

3. The average number of methods per class should be less than 20. Bigger averages indicate too much responsibility in too few classes.

4. The average number of instance variables per class should be less than six. Similar in reasoning as the previous point.

5. The average number of comment lines should be greater than one. Smaller averages indicate too little documentation with the (small) methods.

H.1.2 Other Experiences

The following numbers are from a talk Tom Love gave at the Object-World '91 conference and are based on his experiences from working with a number of companies on O-O development efforts:

1. A prototype class has 10 to 15 methods, each with 5 to 10 lines of code, and takes one person-week to develop.

2. A production class has 20 to 30 methods, each with 10 to 20 lines of code, and takes eight person-weeks to develop. In both these cases, development includes documentation and testing.

3. C++ will have two to three times the lines of code of Smalltalk.

4. Code volume will expand in the first half of the project and decline in the second half, as reviews clean up the system.

H.2 PROBLEM REPORT REQUIREMENTS

During the design and test phase, both developers and testers are going to be finding problems with the system. This section briefly discusses the types of information you will want to capture in tracking these problems. Many of these will be the same for any system development effort. The main difference is the types of objects associated with a problem.

The following is a strawman set of Problem Reporting System (PRS) requirements.

> **Note:** Some goals, such as ease of use (e.g., using the current object as the target of the problem report) and ease of unique Program Trouble Report (PTR) number assignment (e.g., initials + julian date + elapsed seconds) are not listed. As many fields as possible should be filled in automatically for the user.

1. The PRS will work across a LAN, centralized on a server. It is important in this dynamic development environment to make the

PRS as integrated, fast, and seamless as possible. Any objects, including projects down to methods, should be able to be tagged with a problem report.

2. Problem report statuses will be:
   a. Open
   b. Fixing *or* invalid
   c. Fixed
   d. Ready to build
   e. Ready to test (built)
   f. Closed *or* rejected (by originator)
      Note: A *Rejected* status next becomes a *Fixing* status.
      The *Closed* status will have a code associated:
      1) Duplicate (invalid)
      2) Operator error (invalid)
      3) Code fixed (valid)
      4) Documentation fixed (valid)
         The detailed information being kept is important both during and after development to perform *causal analyses* on the data. This is critical in order to improve the quality of the process and product.

   The dates of the status changes and who changed them will be kept.

3. People assigned to a PTR will be notified across the LAN when the PTR is created.

4. Text areas for the problem description and fix description will be available.

5. The name of the person creating the PTR will be kept.

6. It will be possible to search/filter based on criteria such as title, status, or close code.

7. The affected classes for a PTR will be kept.

8. Reports will be possible, based on filter criteria.

9. An indication of a "documentation hit" will be possible.

10. The driver the PTR is fixed in will be kept.

11. Timestamps will be kept on actions.

12. Associated change groups will have PTR numbers included in them.

13. Dependencies between PTR fixes or line items will be kept.

14. Severity level:
   a. Catastrophic—Nothing works, system crashes
   b. Severe—Some areas don't work
   c. Functional—A certain function doesn't work
   d. Minor—A functional improvement, slight problem
   e. Cosmetic—Spelling, appearance

Note: *Functional* is the default level.

Note: The complete preceding text (or something like it) should be shown on the PTR form.

15. PTR Type:
   a. Development
   b. System test
   c. Function test
   d. Unit test

Note: *Development* is the default level.

Appendix I

Measurements
and Metrics

Measuring the wrong thing serves no purpose. Most people would agree that lines of code (LOC) have little or no meaning, due to variations in types of language (2GL vs. 3GL vs. 4GL vs. 5GL . . .), code complexity (loading database fields vs. imaging vs. signal processing vs. differential equations . . .), and *reuse*. I emphasize the word *reuse* because it is especially important for this discussion.

We must focus on what we are trying to achieve, and set up our measurements accordingly. What are we trying to achieve by measuring LOC? Do we really want people to produce more code? *No*, of course not. We want *as little code as necessary to meet our functional requirements*. This should result in the least cost for that function (at least over time — there may be some additional cost for reuse the *first* time, with many subsequent paybacks).

I.1 REUSE

One of the things we must measure is *reuse*. This reuse comes in two flavors:

1. Suppliers of reusable components.
2. Users of reusable components.

Both types of reuse should be measured (and rewarded).
It is important to measure:

1. Successful requests (found the desired functional component).
2. Unsuccessful requests (looked for a function, but did not find one suitable).
3. *Actual uses* of a component, once retrieved (possibly verified a few days after its retrieval via a message to the user).

This information is invaluable for a number of reasons:

1. The usage of a component (or lack of usage) indicates what components should be kept in the reuse library (and which should be removed).
2. The failed requests indicate what components should be built and added to the reuse library.

I.2 METRICS RULES OF THUMB

In planning for new code development (after failing to find a suitable reusable component), the focus should be on the *function* to be delivered. Note that this is not function *points*. The *function* estimates can be based on the identified classes and responsibilities. Since a single method should provide a single service and methods are grouped into contracts, we can use the method "service" groups (contracts) to measure function being delivered. If you really love to count lines, you also know that the average method size is small, so your LOC estimates should be reasonably close. Remember not to fool yourself about the accuracy of these numbers—that's part of the point of this whole change in the way we do business: *We don't* know with great accuracy what we're building!

There are no "right" answers for what information to collect on your project or how to interpret the results. The following rules of thumb will give you some guidelines. The "rules" are the result of O-O project experiences over the last few years, as well as conferences and research detailed in journals. Since LOC metrics are language dependent, two languages will be covered here: Smalltalk and C++. Ratios to derive metrics for other languages are left to the reader.

I.2.1 Design Metrics

These items relate to measuring the quality of designs.

1. *The **average method size** should be less than 8 LOC for Smalltalk and 24 LOC for* C + + *. Bigger averages indicate O-O design problems (i.e. function-oriented coding).*

Watch the average method size. A large or growing number is a warning sign of poor O-O designs. You may want your better O-O designers to hold more reviews with your less O-O experienced folks. Reviews will usually result in code reduction.

My experiences from multiple Smalltalk projects is that the average number of lines of code per method should typically be in the range of 6–10. Better O-O designers typically have averages toward the lower end of the range.

Another way to look at the method size is statements. If you use average statements, your sizes should average less than 5 statements per method for Smalltalk and 15 for C++. Again, larger averages indicate O-O design problems.

2. *The **average number of methods per class** should be less than 20. Bigger averages indicate too much responsibility in too few classes.*

Too many methods in a single class (not counting inherited methods) is a warning sign that too much responsibility is being placed in one type of object. There are probably other undiscovered classes or misplaced responsibilities. Look carefully at the method names and ask yourself questions such as: "Is this something I would expect this class to do?"; "Is there a less obvious class, such as an event, that has not been defined?"

Across multiple O-O development efforts in Smalltalk (each one having hundreds of classes and thousands of methods), my experience has been that the average number of methods per class should typically be in the range of 12–20.

3. *The **average number of instance variables per class** should be less than 6. Similar in reasoning as the previous point— more instance variables indicate that one class is doing more than it should.*

Keep the real world model in mind. An object has attributes that will map to instance variables. Relationships to other system objects will result in additional instance variables. If an object of a certain type would not be expected to know about another object, you don't need another in- stance variable. Part of the way O-O helps deal with complexity is letting relatively independent objects deal with their own concerns and use other objects in a black box fashion. Don't circumvent this benefit by making large, complex objects. Small objects are the desired norm.

4. *The **class hierarchy nesting level** should be less than 6. Start counting at the level of any framework classes that you use or the root class if you don't.*

Greater levels of nesting result in more and more difficulties in testing and are generally not necessary. Larger nesting numbers flag potential design problems. Watch for overzealous object creation. This is almost the opposite concern of having too many methods and/or instance variables.

5. *The **number of subsystem-to-subsystem relationships** should be less than the average number of class-to-class relationships within a subsystem.*

This item relates to low coupling across subsystems. Since the grouping of classes into subsystems is along functionally-related boundaries, this should happen automatically. This low coupling is necessary to allow relatively independent development of subsystems, which may occur in parallel by different small teams or sequentially by the same team.

If you have a lot of message traffic at the subsystem level, the classes probably need to be regrouped or the class design improved.

6. *The **number of class-to-class relationships** within a subsystem should be relatively high.*

This item relates to high cohesion of classes grouped in the same subsystem. If one or more classes within a subsystem don't interact with many of the other classes, they might be better placed in another subsystem or on their own outside the subsystem.

7. *The **instance variable usage** by the methods within a class can be used to look for possible design problems.*

If groups of methods in a class use different sets of instance variables, look closely to see if the class should be split into multiple classes along those "service" lines. Perhaps the sets of methods logically relate to different objects in the problem domain.

8. *The **average number of comment lines** should be greater than 1. Smaller averages indicate too little documentation with the (small) methods.*

Even though the methods are small, they should still have at least one line that describes what they do, along with who wrote it (but I won't get into standards here!).

9. *The **number of problem reports per class** should be low.*

A large number of problem reports indicates analysis and/or design problems, as you would expect. An increase in the number of problem reports indicates unfulfilled requirements.

Encapsulation is wonderful in that it lets us revamp a poorly-built class without rippling changes throughout the system. Don't be afraid to aggressively attack a class that is causing you problems.

It may be that the person that owns the class in question has not fully adjusted to the new paradigm, is not good at extracting abstractions. . . . This measurement should be used in a positive way—to invest in your people as appropriate.

Another factor to look at is your testing methods. Class-level function testing should have fully exercised the class' interface (public protocols). Are certain types of tests not being done? Is the class being used in unexpected ways that are placing new requirements on it?

Problem reports per public method (contract) will help you further isolate exactly what portion of a class is the culprit.

10. *The **number of times a class is reused** across the original application and in other applications might indicate a need to redesign it.*

Count the number of times a class is reused in different applications. If it is not being reused, does it need rework? Abstract classes should be especially good candidates for reuse, since they collect general, common behavior.

11. *The **number of classes and methods thrown away** should occur at a steady rate throughout most of the development process.*

If this is not occurring, then you are probably doing an incremental development instead of performing true iterations on areas of the system. You are probably not pulling out problem domain abstractions along the way either.

I know of at least one O-O company that uses this metric as an indication of projects going awry. This item is a bit of a cross between design and project metrics.

I.2.2 Project Completion Metrics

These items are used to help measure a project's progress toward a complete system. Each project will contribute these (and other) measurements to the company's database to help estimate and track future projects.

Completion of class iterations is the primary focus for project progress measurements. These measurements help resolve staffing and other estimates.

1. **Average number of support classes per key class.**

   Once you have done your initial domain analysis and proto- typing and have a good initial understanding of the application requirements, you will have defined the key classes in the prob- lem domain.

   You can then use the number of key classes to estimate the number of peripheral "support" classes per key class, on average. This will help you estimate the total number of classes in the final system.

2. **Average man-days per application class.**

   Using the total number of application classes that were esti- mated (support classes plus key classes), you can then estimate the amount of human resource you need to complete the project.

3. **Average number of classes per developer.**

   This metric will help you decide what staffing level is needed to develop the application.

4. **Number of major iterations.**

   This metric will help you schedule times when early-release drivers can be given to customers and human factors staff to verify requirements and usability.

5. The **number of subsystems** should relate to major functionally- related portions of the total business' system.

A subsystem should be small enough to be developed by a small, rel- atively independent team (less than 10 developers).

As your iterations take place, keep track of:

1. The number of classes completed

   A class is complete when it meets all requirements.

2. The number of contracts completed

   The contracts should be tracked at a class and subsystem level.

Application size

You can estimate your production application size by multiplying the number of expected instances of a class kept in the image at a given time (vs. on disk) by the size of the class data. Add up all of your classes in this way and you get an estimate of the size of your application. If you are using Smalltalk/V PM, you would then add in the runtime DLL size to get a final number.

I.3 OTHER EXPERIENCES

The following numbers are from a talk Tom Love gave at the Object-World '91 conference and are based on his experiences from working with a number of companies on O-O development efforts. I present them here as another data point. The numbers agree in some instances and disagree in others with the numbers I have given above.

1. A prototype class has 10 to 15 methods, each with 5 to 10 lines of code, and takes 1 person-week to develop.
2. A production class has 20 to 30 methods, each with 10 to 20 lines of code, and takes 8 person-weeks to develop.

    In both these cases, development includes documentation and testing.
3. C++ will have 2 to 3 times the lines of code of Smalltalk.
4. Code volume will expand in the first half of the project and decline in the second half, as reviews clean up the system.

I.4 METRIC STANDARDS

The guidelines above will hopefully help you with your estimating and productivity and quality measurement. Over time there will emerge a useful set of standard measurements that work. There is some excellent work going on at MIT[1] on defining metrics for O-O designs. A few pieces of information gleaned from the metrics research:

1. Deeply nested classes are more complex, due to inheritance.

    The number of instance variables and methods can become quite large (triple digits). This implies more required knowledge in order to test a class and more testing required to verify the class.
2. A class or group of classes (e.g., a framework) with a low amount of coupling to other classes will be more reusable.

    Coupling here means message sends to classes outside the grouping and affects encapsulation and rippling of changes (higher coupling results in lower encapsulation and higher volatility to change).
3. A class has higher cohesion if its methods utilize similar sets of instance variables.

---

[1]Shyam R. Chidamber and Chris F. Kemerer, "Towards a metrics suite for object-oriented design," OOPSLA '91 Conference Proceedings, October 1991, pp. 197–211.

It is an interesting idea that if you see that a class' methods don't use the same variables, the design may be improved by splitting the class up into multiple classes. This can be used as another indicator of a class design that should be looked at more closely.

The area of metrics is still young. For now, we have rules of thumb to follow. We'll have to wait for more rigorous rules and standard measures for an O-O design.

I.5 METRICS FORM

The following form is suggested for your use in recording your project information. This type of information needs to be collected via a metrics tool.

(1) Overall:

Type of application (graphics, accounts receivable, editing . . .):

_____

_____

_____

Target: internal _____ external _____

Length of project: _____ years _____ months

     Complete_____ Underway _____ Cancelled _____

Development process (check one)

     iterative _____ incremental _____ waterfall _____

     Tools used:

_____

_____

_____

_____ total # application classes
_____ total # modified base classes
_____ total man-months
_____ # major iterations on the project
_____ total LOC
_____ total statements
_____ total comment lines
_____ deepest hierarchy nesting
_____ # "key" classes (central to the project)
_____ # "peripheral" (support) classes

_____ (estimated) Classes thrown away
_____ (estimated) Methods thrown away

Code delivery:

Primary language: _____
Other languages used:

_____

_____ Non-primary language LOC
Why did you need this (vs. using
one language exclusively)?

_____
_____
_____
_____

_____ % source included
_____ % object code only

Team size:

_____ # developers
_____ # testers
_____ # information developers
_____ # human factors

Averages:

_____ average method size (LOC)
_____ average # methods/class
_____ average # instance variables/class
_____ average man-days per class
_____ average # major iterations/class
_____ average number of classes/person
Did you have more than
one person/class?   yes _____   no _____

Percentages:

_____ % man-days in analysis
_____ % man-days in design
_____ % man-days in coding
_____ % man-days in testing
_____ % man-days in documentation

Types of classes:

_____ % new   _____ % modified
_____ % abstract   _____ % concrete
_____% relatively well understood at start
_____% not understood at the beginning

Comments:

_____

_____

_____

_____

_____

_____

_____

_____

_____

(1) Per class:

Type of class - new _____   modified _____
(check one/line)
                    abstract _____   concrete _____
                         key _____   support _____
              well understood _____   not _____

_____ # major iterations
_____ # problem reports
_____ project % complete when created
_____ # (re)uses
_____ # subclasses

Appendix J

Coding Standards

I have recommended that you give your developers some guidelines to help with good coding practices. The objective in creating coding conventions is to be able to develop code that is readable, maintainable, and extensible.[1] Use of these conventions will help accomplish this objective.

> **Note:** The same terms that have been used throughout the rest of this book are used here. Where appropriate, substitute the corresponding terms for C++. For example, *members* and *member functions* can be substituted for *instance variables* and *methods*, respectively.

In order to help you define conventions for your project, this section presents something to start with in general, followed by specifics for two major O-O languages: Smalltalk and C++. In a recent survey of who is using what O-O language, C++ ranked first, followed by

---

[1]Thanks to all those I worked with over the last few years who helped to document a usable, useful set of conventions!

Smalltalk and Objective-C.[2] As in most debates, there are advocates for each of these languages, as well as others. Debates of the pros and cons of pure versus hybrid languages can be found in numerous places, including Stroustrup's book on C++, Meyer's book on Eiffel, and articles such as "The Real Advantages of Pure Object-Oriented Systems or Why Object-Oriented Extensions to C are Doomed to Fail," by LaLonde et al.

J.1.1 Smalltalk versus C++

I will briefly compare the two languages before getting into the straw-man standards.

1. Memory management

Subjective Range

|⊢──────────────────────────────⊣|

Better →

C++   ST

    Smalltalk: the system handles memory allocation and freeing for you.

    C++: the programmer must worry about the details of creating and freeing memory and finding any mistakes.

2. Tools/Environment

Subjective Range

|⊢──────────────────────────────⊣|

Better →

C++   ST

    Smalltalk: has an integrated hierarchy browser, object debugger, dynamic "compiler," and workspaces.

    C++: compiler and linker with a separate debugger.

3. Learning curve

Subjective Range

|⊢──────────────────────────────⊣|

Better →

ST   C++

    Smalltalk: forces a totally new paradigm.

    C++: plus - similar to C; minus - similar to C. May be easier to learn the syntax, but more difficult to learn the new paradigm.

---

[2]Leslie Hellanack, "IDC's First Object Technology Survey," *First Class*, (September/October 1991), pp. 14–15.

4. Performance

Subjective Range

Better →

ST   C++

Smalltalk: most of the time, meets requirements. Sometimes, you may need to rewrite selected portions in C++ or assembler.

  C++: somewhat faster production code, on average.

5. Object-orientedness

Subjective Range

Better →

C++   ST

Smalltalk: as pure as it gets.

  C++: mix of O-O and non-O-O parts. Handles key O-O requirements: classes, inheritance, and polymorphism.

6. Flexibility

Subjective Range

Better →

ST   C++

Smalltalk: enforces O-O paradigm.

  C++: too many handguns for programmers to accidentally kill their project with, such as violating encapsulation, in-line code causing numerous recompiles, and so on. Does have some nice features, such as "totally private" data and functions.

7. Multiple inheritance

Subjective Range

Better →

(the debate continues)

Smalltalk: ain't got it.

  C++: got it.

8. Available classes

Subjective Range

Better →

C++   ST

Smalltalk: hundreds of solid classes for most common areas, used for years. Some newer classes in areas such as DBCS.

  C++: some relatively new libraries are available.

9. Maintenance

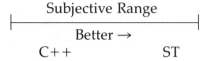

Smalltalk: enforced encapsulation, a simple paradigm of messaging objects, and a simple syntax, with an extensible language, make maintenance easier.

C++: hard to read and understand. Pitfalls due to flexibility can become a nightmare. Changes are more likely to ripple (e.g., due to use of friend functions).

10. Integration

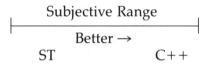

Smalltalk: portable, but less than C. More work required to work with packages geared for C, like Presentation Manager

C++: portable, sort of. If no advantage is made of platform specifics, then the code is portable. Works well with system components like Presentation Manager.

NET: Both languages have a place in the O-O world.

J.2 COMMON CODING STANDARDS

J.2.1 Naming Conventions

I can't emphasize enough that the names you give to classes, methods, instance variables, and formal parameters are *very important*. Having debates about what to name something is not a waste of time. Usually, if you are having a discussion about what the name should be, you need some more problem-domain understanding and/or design sessions.

Use of plural forms of names where collections of objects are kept, type information at the highest abstract level possible in formal parameters, and logical consistency of method names all contribute to the readability and understandability of the system. *Print* should mean what its name implies, no matter what the object and *aString* tells me what type to expect.

The difference between good naming and bad is the difference between an understandable system (for the developers *and* the users!)

and one that is not. Don't cripple the real-world modelling benefits of object technology by poor names of model or UI objects.

1. Instance variables and temporary variables
    a. All instance variable and temporary (local) variable names will begin with a lowercase letter. After the initial lowercase letter, words will be identified by capitalizing the first letter of each word. For example, *accountNumber.*
2. Formal parameters
    a. All formal parameter names will begin with 'a' or 'an.' After this initial word, all following words will be identified by capitalizing the first letter of each word. For example, *aWithdrawal-Transaction.*
    b. All parameter names will reflect their expected type. For example, *anAccount.*
3. Classes
    a. All class names will begin with a three-letter prefix. (For example, 'Atm' for the ATM application classes, such as *Atm-Account,* or 'Fnb' for the First National Bank's classes.) This prefix identifies the originator. This is important when installing code from outside and is also important when delivering code to your customers. You want to minimize the chances of having class name collisions.

        Note that if you have two classes with the same name (other than the unique three-letter prefix), you need to look at what they are doing. Either they should be the same class or one is misnamed.

J.2.2 Indentation and Spacing

1. In general, only one statement will be coded per line.
2. Avoid coding lines that are too long to fit within the boundaries of a typical editor. A rule of thumb is a maximum of around 70 characters per line.
3. Code will be indented one tab stop and will begin one tab from the left margin. Nested code will be indented to convey to the reader of the code that it is nested, using one tab for each additional nesting level.
4. Logical blocks of code may have a blank line before and after.

J.2.3 Exception Handling

You should plan ahead for exceptions. In Smalltalk, for example, you do not want to get a "Does not understand" walkback in a product.

You probably want a logging capability to aid your support people (the developers!).

For C++, I'd recommend reading "Exception Handling for C++" by Andrew Koenig and Bjarne Stroustrup.[3]

J.3 SMALLTALK CODING STANDARDS

Only those conventions specific to Smalltalk will be listed here. See Appendix J.2, "Common Coding Standards," for additional standards.

J.3.1 Naming Conventions

1. Formal parameters
   a. All parameter names will reflect their expected type. For example, *anAccount*. Be careful not to overqualify the parameter, thereby assuming a particular implementation. For instance, *aCollection* may be better than *anOrderedCollection* if any type of collection can be passed to the method.
2. Global variables
   a. All global variable names will have the three-letter prefix, as described previously for class-naming conventions.
3. Pool dictionaries ("constants")
   a. All constant names will have the three-letter prefix, as described previously for class-naming conventions.

J.3.2 Accessing Methods

1. Accessing methods will be named *instVarName* and *instVarName:* (i.e., no 'set' or 'get' in the name). For example, for an instance variable named *balance*, data-accessing methods should be named *balance* and *balance*.
2. Accessing methods should be created only for those instance variables that are to be accessible from outside the object. *Don't break the encapsulation except where necessary!*

   There is a design trade-off to be made for accessing object data from *within* the object's methods. It is certainly faster to directly access the variable. However, some changes in the way the object is designed can cause ripples for direct access. For example, if the data are now computed instead of kept around, all direct-access code must be updated. Another benefit of accessing methods is that laissez-faire initialization at access time can be

---

[3]Andrew Koenig and Bjarne Stroustrup, "Exception Handling for C++," *Journal of Object-Oriented Programming*, (July/August 1990), pp. 16–33.

done (i.e., check for nil and set a default value, if necessary, before continuing). Yet another possible benefit of accessing methods is additional capabilities, such as business rule enforcement, since all data are accessed through methods.

J.3.3 Indentation and Spacing

1. In general, only one cascaded statement will be coded per line. (An exception is very short message names such as 'cr' for the Transcript window.)

```
——————————— CASCADED MESSAGES EXAMPLE ———————————


    ( receiver )
     firstMessage;
     secondMessage;
     . . .
     lastMessage.
```

2. Blocks will be laid out as shown in the following examples (or combinations thereof).

```
——————————— IFTRUE:IFFALSE: BLOCKS ———————————


    ( condition )
     ifTrue: [
       theFirstTrueStatement.
       theLastTrueStatement.
     ]
     ifFalse: [
       theFirstFalseStatement.
       theLastFalseStatement.
     ].
```

```
——————————— OTHER BLOCKS ———————————


    ( collectionExpression )
        do: [ :each | aOneLineBlock ].

    ( collectionExpression )
        do: [ :each |
          firstStatement.
```

```
        lastStatement.
        ].

[ booleanExpression ] whileTrue: [
        firstTrueStatement.
        lastTrueStatement.
        ].
```

The layout is a balance between readability, compactness, and ease of change. Remember, a *lot* of your time will be spent *reading* code and you have a relatively small piece of screen real estate to do it in. Also, you want it to be easy to add and delete lines anywhere in the block, including at the end.

3. A blank line should not be left between the method selector line and the method comment.

4. Method comments should be indented two tabs from the left margin so that they are clearly set off from the method selector (above) and the method code (below).

5. Leave one blank line between the end of the comments and the temporary variable definitions, or start of code (if there are no temporary variables).

6. Temporary variables (if any) will begin at the first tab position.

7. Spaces will be placed in the following locations:
   a. Before and after an assignment operator.
   b. Before and after a binary message selector.
   c. Between a keyword message and its argument.
   d. Before and after a quoted string. (Exception: When doing string concatenation, a space is not required preceding the comma used for concatenation.)
   e. After the opening '|' for temporary variables and before the closing '|'.
   f. Before a block variable name and its leading colon, and after its name.
   g. Before and after the outermost layer of a parenthesized conditional expression.
   h. After the opening '#(' and before the closing ')' of a constant collection.

J.3.4 Comments

1. Class comments
   a. Each class will have a short description of its purpose, each class variable, and each instance variable in a class method called *classComment*.
2. Method comments
   a. Each method will have a short description of its purpose, an indication of who created it (and when), and (in a separate file or at the bottom of methods) a description of modifications made to it (including by whom and when). This information should be cleaned up for each product release, with one line showing the owner's name and product release date remaining.
   b. *Private* or *Public* should appear at the beginning of the comment for methods to indicate their intended use. (*Private* is to be used for methods that you do not expect to be referenced from other objects; i.e., they are only to be called from other methods within their class. *Public* is to be used for methods that are allowed to be referenced from outside this class.)
   c. Optionally, text can be included in the comments that can be selected for execution (e.g., example of the use of this method).
3. Code comments
   a. Comments that provide an explanation or clarification of the code within the method can be placed above the code, or at the end of the lines within the code. If placed above the code, the comment should begin at the same indentation as the code itself. If placed on the line of code, the comment should be located far enough to the right so that it does not interfere with reading of the actual code.
4. Code change comments
   a. Changes made as a result of a Program Trouble Report (PTR) will be recorded as comments. The comments will contain the change number (providing a reference to the description of the problem), a description of the change, a date stamp, and an indication of the person making the change. Descriptions of changes for a method will not be kept at the beginning of the method, which would require scrolling to see the active code.[4] They will be kept at the end or in a separate location.

---

[4]Tools could provide much of the support for change notes and documentation, separate from the active method code.

b. Individual code that is changed will not be flagged with a change indicator, since properly designed methods should be very short.

5. In general, code that is commented out (i.e., not compiled) will not be submitted for a build (i.e., no in-line archival). If code *is* commented out (e.g., due to temporary fix), it will not be left for more than one build cycle.

J.3.5 Miscellaneous Guidelines

1. Methods that have no explicit need to return a value should return *self*. This results in more useful data being available to the debugger, should the need arise.

2. When appropriate, use *ifFalse:* or *whileFalse:* instead of using *not*.

3. Periods should appear at the end of all statements. This includes the last statement in a method or a block. Using periods will help with future modifications to the method, when code is to be added at the end.

   Note: There are instances where Smalltalk will not allow a period on the last statement in a block. However, it is preferable to use the periods, and it should be done where possible.

4. Each class should have an 'example' class method defined, which performs functions illustrating the class, if it makes sense to perform the function of that class individually. The first method comment line should allow execution of the example, such as *"ExampleClass example."*

   Note: Each class comment may also contain a copyright statement.

J.4 C++ CODING STANDARDS

Good practices in C are still good in C++. For example, good use of indentation and alignment of block delimiters is the same. I'm not going to go into great depth on the base language. By now, you should have good rules to follow. What I *will* do is give you advice about the "++" part of the language.

J.4.1 Naming Conventions

Since C++ code consists of a mixture of O-O and function-oriented syntax, you might consider adding the characters "Obj" to the end of the name of variables that refer to class instances. In this way, a developer looking at the code could readily differentiate the objects from the function-oriented variables.

J.4.2 Accessing Methods

1. Member accessing methods will be named *memberName*. For example, for a class's member (instance variable) named *balance*, a data accessing member function (method) should be named *balance*.

2. Accessing methods should be created only for those members that are to be accessible from outside the object. *Don't break the encapsulation except where necessary!*

   There is a design trade-off to be made for accessing object data from *within* the class's functions. It is certainly faster to directly access the member. However, some changes in the way the class is designed can cause ripples for direct access. For example, if the data are now computed instead of kept around, all direct-access code must be updated. Another benefit of accessing functions is that laissez-faire initialization at access time can be done (i.e., check for a valid value and set a default, if necessary, before continuing). Yet another possible benefit of accessing functions is additional capabilities, such as business rule enforcement, since all data are accessed through functions.

J.4.3 Comments

See Appendix J.4.4, "Miscellaneous Guidelines," for a template showing suggested locations for class and method comments.

J.4.4 Miscellaneous Guidelines

1. Avoid friend functions.

   One of the benefits of O-O is data hiding (encapsulation). Another is real-world modeling. *Friend functions* break the rules of encapsulation by allowing methods outside the class to access its data. This will cause future changes to ripple through more code. These functions also have no direct correlation with anything in the real world — actions don't take place without a corresponding object. I've never seen an example of the use of friend functions across classes that I didn't think could be better handled with another class. And the maintenance headaches . . . . With friends like these, who needs enemies?

   There are times where friend functions are necessary, due to the way the language is defined. For example, in order to overload common operators such as + while allowing commutivity, friend functions are necessary. However, in these cases, I would highly recommend that the function be defined in one class only (versus across multiple classes).

2. Avoid in-line functions.

The biggest problem for C++ programmers today is massive recompilations. *In-line functions* make the need for recompiles (versus relinking only) more likely to occur. Nobody needs a little extra speed that badly — remember that *people* are more expensive than *machines*. Save the tuning for later, and then only if necessary. If you get to the point where you think in-line functions are necessary, then you may want to rethink your hardware platform target or write small portions in assembly language. The latter choice will make portability more difficult.

3. Do not declare members (instance variables) as *public.*

One of the strengths of O-O is data hiding (encapsulation). Do not willingly violate your objects' privacy! The public area should only contain the *contract protocol* that the class is set up to provide services for.

4. Only have *Protected* functions for abstract classes.

This will ensure that the functions are only available to derived classes (subclasses), in case someone erroneously tries to create an instance of the class.

5. Use explicit tags for function scoping.

Don't rely on the default. Include all three types, even if one or more are empty. Developers will have an easier time if they consistently see the same format. Include end-of-line divider comments to help readability. Put constructor and destructor functions first in the public section, even if they're empty.

The following template is offered as a starting point to refine to suit your team's style:

C++ CODING TEMPLATE

```
// <classname> .hxx   <comment on class(es) contained>
#include <whatever needed>
// <comment on class 1's purpose, collaborators,
// clients, owner>
class <class1name>
{
private:                    //-------- Private area --------
  static <classvar1 decl> // CLASS: <comment on classvar1>
    <var1 decl>            // <comment on (inst)var1>
    <funct1 decl>          // <comment on funct1>
```

```
protected:                  //-------- Protected area--------
   static <classvar2 decl> // CLASS: <comment on classvar2>
   <var2 decl>             // <comment on var2>
   <funct2 decl>           // <comment on funct2>

public:           //-------- public area --------
<class1name>      // CONSTRUCTOR: <comment on
                                     constructor>
<class1name>      // DESTRUCTOR:<comment on destructor>
<funct3 decl>     // <comment on funct3>
}
                  //-------- External area --------
<funct4 decl>     // <comment on funct4>
```

6. Put all declarations at the start of their scoping area.

Even though you can scatter declarations at will, remember readability. Put variable declarations that are used throughout a function at the top of the function; put loop variable declarations within the start of the loop code.

7. Functions that allocate objects should destroy them.

If possible, the function that invokes *new* should also invoke *delete*. Humans are not good at storage management. Orphans will eventually bite you . . . and the cause won't be easy to track down.

8. Use *const.*

Whenever your design intentions are to leave a parameter unmolested, put the design information into the code via the *const* declaration. Even though the compiler will not refuse to compile the code if you violate your intentions, at least you will get a warning and can consciously decide what actions to take.

9. The same name should mean the same thing.

Be careful with your overloading of operators and naming of member functions. Use of the same name should have an obvious relation to the previous use(s) of the name. For example, using a " + " operation on two *Account* objects might return the sum of the balances of the two accounts. The same operation on two *Circle* objects might return a circle with a radius equal to the sum of the two arguments' radii. Sending a " + " to a *Car* object and getting back its list of add-on features would not fit the metaphor of what "+" means elsewhere (however, *adding a new feature* might work with a "+" operator!).

10. Declare base classes public when deriving new (sub)classes.

There are times when you would like to keep tight rein on class contents. However, it will normally make sense for derived (sub)classes to have access to *protected and public* and clients to have access to *public* areas of the base class(es).

11. Call virtual class constructors in derived class constructors.

I pity the poor fools who have to spend nights and weekends searching for the reason that a class variable occasionally takes on strange, unexpected values . . . only to find through their bleary eyes that they forgot to allocate space for a virtual base (super) class, so that storage is allocated for the base class's members. Even if the class has no members, declare it—you never know what future changes will come back to haunt you (or the person who inherits your mine field)!

12. Don't mix class pointers.

Mixing pointers can come back to haunt you. For example, casting a base class address as a derived class pointer can cause subsequent changes to unintended data areas. Also, developers are not going to be able to read code where base class pointers are used to point to derived class(es), even though this will work.

13. Put error logging code in base class virtual functions.

Something like:

```
cerr < < "BASE_CLASS_NAME received FUNCTION_NAME,";
cerr < < "which should be implemented by my derived class(es)";
exit(1);
```

will do the trick. You can certainly define your own actions that utilize your project's error conventions. The reason I don't recommend initializing the virtual function to zero is that derived (sub)classes will be virtual also if the function is not overridden. This punishes developers that might wish to do more "exploratory" programming—they may not need that function in the subclass yet and don't want to have to declare all the functions up front. This is probably my Smalltalk bias showing through. Since the *compiler* catches an attempt to instantiate a virtual class, you may want to override me and set the virtual functions to zero.

14. Overload $>>$ and $<<$

Standard I/O should be facilitated for new types of objects wherever possible.

J.4.5 My Two Cents' Worth

I can't close a section on C++ without making some comments. I will frankly admit up front that I am a fan of Smalltalk (not a surprise at this point!).

Point 1: I would warn you that there are a lot of C programmers out there using C++. By this, I mean that O-O is a paradigm shift. If you take someone and give them extensions to their current language, still allowing them to go about business as usual, don't expect them to have an easier time of it. They will certainly have an easier time learning the new syntax and be able to crank out code faster . . . *but* they will take *longer* to truly move to O-O and the benefits of the new technology. If you are going to use a hybrid language like C++, I would make two recommendations:

1. Make sure you use an O-O methodology religiously and make sure that the resulting design makes it effectively into the code (as verified by O-O experts).

2. Get training on Smalltalk and use it for a time to force the paradigm shift. While it is possible to write function-oriented code in Smalltalk, it is more difficult than in C++.

Point 2: *C++ is more difficult than C—not less—for the class developers.* It is true that the clients of the code, if it is done well, have an easy time of it, but what group spends their time living within the constraints of an off-the-shelf framework? The clients will soon want new derived (sub)classes, new methods to existing classes, and so on and will delve into the greater complexity that is C++. By defining and following some conventions, you can help manage this complexity.

Point 3: The debate continues to rage about multiple inheritance. If you feel the need and desire to use it and the language supports it, have at it. My experience has been that it is not necessary and adds complexity to the system. A small example: a student is also an instructor at a university. You might want a *StudentInstructor* class to be defined that has the *Student* and *Instructor* classes as base (super) classes. There are a number of alternatives that don't use multiple inheritance. For example, a *Person* class could contain a collection of *classesTaken* and *classesTaught*. You could also define *role* objects.

J.4.6 Porting C to C++

These points are basic guidelines to follow to migrate your C code to C++.[5] They don't guarantee that you won't have other bugs due to the change in language, but they will handle the most common types of changes necessary.

J.4.6.1 Pre-ANSI C to ANSI C

1. Declare function prototypes in your class definition (.cxx or .cpp) files.

2. Modify the function definitions to fit the new format in your include (.hxx or .hpp) files.

3. Rewrite any code with low-level assumptions. For example, rewrite any routines that assume the position of parameters on the stack, since this will change under the ANSI compiler.

J.4.6.2 ANSI C to ANSI C++

1. Rename any variables that coincide with C++ keywords, such as *new, delete, this,* and *friend.*

2. Rename variables as necessary so that *struct* names and other variable names do not match. In C, this was allowed, but in C ++ it is not (since there is only one name space).

3. Look at your C libraries as well as your code—they will probably require some of the preceding changes as well.

---

[5]This discussion is adapted from notes taken during a talk given by Steve Blaha on 11/22/91.

Appendix K.

An Exercise for the Reader

In order to get the ball rolling, I'll briefly describe a personal scheduler application here. You can use this as the basis for following along with the text to develop a useful application of moderate size.

K.1 PERSONAL SCHEDULER REQUIREMENTS

The following requirements are offered as a starting point in the development effort. Any vagueness in the description will have to be worked out with your "users."

PERSONAL SCHEDULER
INITIAL USER REQUIREMENTS

1. A monthly calendar can be displayed, with an indication of which days have items scheduled on them. The user should be able to directly pick a day to view.
2. A daily calendar can be displayed, with user-defined time slots scheduled. The user should be able to label items with start and stop times.

---

3. Alarms should be able to be set for items, with user-specified number of minutes before the start time, for reminders.
4. A hard-copy printout of the current week's schedule should be printed at user request.
5. A "floating" to-do list is to be carried from day to day, to be shown along with scheduled items as long as they are still open. The to-do items are to be shown in user-defined priority order.

The target operating system and language is not specified in the requirements.

K.2 A SUGGESTED METAPROCESS

I think everyone has an opinion on what they'd like to see in a personal scheduling tool. I'd suggest you get either someone in your group or a willing person from outside your group to play the part of your user. Make sure that your user understands that you need to keep the application reasonably simple, but that the requirements can certainly evolve somewhat during the analysis phase.

While the bulk of your (small) group should be playing the roles of developers, involved in the model class analysis, design, and implementation in the analysis and design phases, someone could be assigned responsibility for the UI classes, playing the role of a human factors person.

You may also want to appoint someone as the technical leader of the effort, with responsibility to organize the iteration scheduling and hold design reviews.

Glossary

Abstract class. A class that has no instances, created to facilitate sharing of state data and services between similar, more specialized subclasses.

Accessing method. A method that facilitates access to an object's state data, either to change or retrieve its state. Generally, the accessing methods are named according to the state data (instance variable). So, *balance* and *balance:* methods would allow an object to retrieve and set the value of an account's balance.

Analysis phase. The portion of the software development effort that focuses on the *problem domain*. Analysis occurs after the first phase: business. The primary product of this effort is a clear statement of the system requirements for the following phase: design and test.

Application. An application in an O-O system is a collection of classes that work together to provide related functionality to the end user. The application consists of model objects and UI objects.

Application class. A class that represents an object in your application's problem domain. For example, an *Account* class would be an application class for the banking industry.

Assessment period. The final period of a major iteration of the IDP. This is the time when the work that has been completed is inspected for criteria such as performance, quality, and reuse.

ATM. Automated Teller Machine. This is the banking application that is used as a sample throughout the book.

Attribute. The information that a class keeps on itself. The class's state data.

Base class. A class, generally included in the environment or purchased externally, which provides non-application capabilities. For example, a *String* class might certainly be used in your application, but is not related to the industry domain.

Behavior. A service provided by a class upon request through a message. A method.

Black box. Viewing something from the outside only. Treating something as a black box means that you don't care how it works inside—you only care that it provides the service you requested.

Build. A minor iteration within the production portion of the IDP. This is the cycle where developers are submitting work completed on scheduled line items to be put into the group software base.

Business phase. The initial software development phase. This is the phase when the initial customer requirements and customer type are described, actual customers to use as partners are found, and initial business concerns, such as profitability and priority, are handled.

Cardinality. The number of expected instances of an object related to another type of object in a diagram. For example, a 1:N relationship between two classes would result in the source class having an instance variable that holds a collection of target class instances in a running system.

Class. A class is a template that defines the structure and capabilities of an object instance. The class definition includes the state data and the behaviors (methods) for the instances of that class. The class can be thought of as a factory, creating instances as needed. For example, an *Account* class may have methods to allow deposits and withdrawals to be made, using a *balance* instance variable to hold the current balance. This definition defines how an Account works, but it is not an actual account.

Client. A requestor of services. When a message is sent to a class requesting a particular service, the class that sent the request is the client and the class that services the request is the server.

Collaborate. To work together to achieve a goal. Classes collaborate by delegating work to the most appropriate classes in order to carry out a requested service for a client. For example, a *withdrawalTransaction* object may request that a *savingsAccount* object make a withdrawal from itself as part of the overall withdrawal actions. Collaboration is a more common form of reuse than inheritance.

Collaboration diagram. A graphical view of an O-O system design, including classes, subsystems groupings, and contract usage.

Concrete class. A class which has instances. For example, there might be a *SavingsAccount* class which has a number of instances in a running application for a bank.

Contract. A simplifying abstraction of a group of related public responsibilities (methods) that are to be provided by subsystems and classes to their clients. For example, *maintain account balances* may be a contract for the *Account* class (and all its subclasses). This contract may be implemented by methods such as *deposit:*, *withdraw:*, and *balance*.

CUA. Common User Access. Software UI standards developed by IBM.

Data dictionary. A document that is used in structured (function-oriented) methodologies to describe the contents of dataflows and datastores.

Dataflow diagram. A diagram used in structured (function-oriented) methodologies to analyze the data movements and processing in the system. The diagram contains processes, dataflows, datastores, and external entities. It does not contain control information.

Datastore. An entity on a dataflow diagram (DFD) that indicates where data come to rest between processes. It is implementation independent—i.e., it is used for all types of data storage—and is used in a structured (function-oriented) methodology.

DBCS. Double Byte Character Set. Two bytes are needed to represent characters in languages such as Japanese.

DDE. Dynamic Data Exchange. A standard protocol for communication between software packages.

DLL. Dynamic Link Library. DLLs are used as resources that load as needed, thus taking up memory only when necessary.

Delegation. Reuse of a class's services through messages versus through inheritance.

Design and test phase. Design is the portion of the software development effort that focuses on the *solution domain*. It occurs after the analysis phase. The primary product of this effort is a software system that accurately models the portion of the business being automated for the final phase: packaging.

Driver. Prerelease, partially functional product code, used for customer and usability testing to verify requirements and improve the UI, respectively.

Dynamic binding. Dynamic binding, also known as *late binding*, associates a variable with an object class *during the system's execution*. This allows the system to dynamically decide what method to use, based on the type of object being dealt with. For example, the *SavingsAccount* and *CDAccount* classes may both have a *withdraw* method, since the bank has different withdrawal policies for the types of accounts. Using dynamic binding (and polymorphism), the system would choose the right method code to execute.

Encapsulation. Data hiding. Objects encapsulate their data, making them accessible *only* through messages to the object.

Framework. An architected group of functions intended to be reused for a specific purpose by many types of users and applications. For example, an application framework could provide many of the general functions of basic menubars, popup dialogs, and so on. By subclassing a new application window class under the framework classes (calling the architected functions and using the architected data), the developer can reuse the basic capabilities and "only" has to develop the application-specific functions.

Hierarchy. A tree structure. For classes, an inheritance structure. For example, *SavingsAccount* and *CheckingAccount* may be subclasses (lower in the hierarchy) of *Account*.

Hierarchy nesting. The number of subclassing levels in the class hierarchy.

IDP. Iterative Development Process. A technique for developing software in an evolutionary, discovery mode, with each major iteration providing inputs to the next. The iterations are composed of planning, production, and assessment periods.

Incremental process. Development steps that result in a piecemeal delivery of application functions over the life of the project. So, a set of end user functions are delivered in driver 1, some additional end user functions are delivered in driver 2, and so on until the entire application has been built.

Information development. The group that produces the end user application documentation, such as the user's manual.

Inheritance. You can organize similar types of classes of objects into categories called class hierarchies. The lower-level classes (called subclasses) can use the services of all the higher classes in their hierarchy. This is called inheritance. Inheritance is simply a way of reusing services and data. For example, Savings accounts are types of general Account, and IRA accounts are types of Savings accounts. The Savings account inherits the capability to handle deposits from the Account class.

Instance. An instance (or just "object") is an actual object, waiting to perform services and holding some state data. For example, a person's account at a bank is an instance of the Account class. It is possible to make deposits and withdrawals, or possibly to ask the account for its current balance. This account shares information (such as methods) with all instances of the same class, but they are *different* objects, with separate state data (such as balance).

Instance variable. A place to store and refer to an object's state data. In traditional systems, this would be a data variable. In O-O systems, data are made up of object instances, so it is called an "instance variable."

Interface coupling. Interclass interactions are via message protocols only (i.e., no manipulation of another class's data, even if you are a subclass of the class).

Internal coupling. Interclass interactions include manipulating another class's data. This can occur in C++ by use of friend functions, or derived (sub)classes if the base (super)class declares the data protected or public. In Smalltalk, subclasses always have access to superclass data; nonsubclasses never have access to a class's data.

Iteration. A single cycle of the IDP. This is also called a *major* iteration, to distinguish it from a build cycle, which is a *minor* iteration of the system. An IDP iteration is generally a multi-month effort to work on a set of product line items.

Iterative process. Development steps that result in multiple deliveries of the same application functions over the life of the project. So, most end user functions are delivered in multiple drivers, with each delivery better than the last.

Key classes. The primary classes necessary to provide solutions to users' needs in a particular area of the business. For example, for an ATM application at a bank, classes such as *Account, Transaction,* and *Customer* are central to the functions being provided, while other support classes, such as *TransactionLog* and *Receipt,* are not as important to provide these functions. Key classes tend to be more stable than other parts of the system.

Line item. A scheduled activity during an iteration. Generally, a functional piece of the system to be worked on by a single individual for a period of time.

Major iteration. A multi-month effort to work on a set of product line items in an iterative development process (IDP).

Message. Objects communicate via messages. In order to request a service from another object, an object sends it a message. This is the only means to get information from an object, since its data are not directly accessible (this is called encapsulation).

Message flow diagram. A time-ordered sequence of message sends between a group of classes or subsystems. Message flows are used for a variety of purposes, including method and use-case design.

Method. A class service or behavior. Methods are executed whenever an object receives a message. They contain the logic, in the form of more message sends, for the objects in a class.

Methodology. A group of activities geared toward achieving a goal. In the case of a software development methodology, the activities describe the steps to take and types of information to collect to facilitate the production of quality software systems.

Model object. An object that simulates something in the business's problem domain. For example, an account is a model object for a bank. The model object classes are relatively stable, since they are fundamental to the way the business works. This is in contrast to a UI object.

O-O. Object-oriented.

Object. An object is anything that models "things" in the real world. These "things" may be physical entities, such as cars, or events, such as a concert, or abstractions, such as a general-purpose account. An object has state (data) and behavior (methods or services), as defined for the *class* of objects it belongs to.

Object-oriented. In this book, object orientation means that classes, objects, inheritance, polymorphism, and encapsulation are used to model problem domains in developing software solutions.

Overload. To use the same name for methods (doing logically the same thing) in different classes. For example, *balance* might be a method in *CDAccount, MutualFundAccount,* and *CheckingAccount* classes. Logically, *balance* means the same thing: "please give me your current balance, whatever that means to an object of your type." (You can imagine the problems understanding a class that used *balance* in a different way!)

Packaging phase. The final software development phase. This is the phase when the software system that has been built is prepared for commercial sale. The system testing is performed, sales avenues are defined, training is prepared, and language translation takes place.

Peripheral class. A class which provides part of the supporting framework for the business' key classes. User interface classes are always support classes.

Persist. To exist outside the system. In many O-O systems, objects are created and destroyed at furious rates. Those that *do* remain around for fairly long times often live precariously in the latest volatile copy of the system environment. Persistent objects are saved outside the system, ready to be recreated when needed. The storage for persistent objects can be system files, O-O DBMSs, traditional DBMSs, or other storage techniques.

Planning period. The initial time period in a major iteration of the IDP. This is the time when schedules are prepared for the production period.

Polymorphism. Polymorphism is the capability of a single variable to refer to different objects that fulfill certain message protocol responsibilities (roles). For example, an instance variable called *myAccount* can hold a *SavingsAccount* or *CDAccount* object at different times. No matter which type of object the variable holds at a given time, it can be sent a *balance* message to retrieve the current balance of the account. Polymorphism, along with dynamic binding, make type-specific coding, such as a *cdBalance* message, unnecessary.

Private method. A method that exists to help *this* class get its work done. It is not available to other classes. (Contrast with public method.)

Problem domain. The area of the business that an application under development is concerned with. For example, the area of a bank's business that has to do with ATMs is the problem domain for an ATM application.

Process. A function. It appears on DFDs in structured (function-oriented) methodologies to indicate some processing of the data shown on the dataflows.

Production period. The middle time period of a major iteration of the IDP. This is the time when software line items are built.

Prototype. A partially functional version of an application.

Public method. A method that is made available to other classes (clients). Public methods are grouped into contracts. (Contrast with private method.)

Requirements document. This is a clear, concise statement of the end users' needs for a product. It contains functions to be provided and no design.

Responsibility. A service that has been assigned to a class, due to client classes' needs. A method is an implementation of a responsibility.

Reuse. The utilization of existing code to satisfy a new requirement. This can come from inheritance, class delegation, library routine access through DLLs, and/or application communication through DDE.

Reuse library. A repository of *solid* reusable components, maintained by its class owners. The company's most important software asset. Reuse across applications should normally be restricted to the reuse library.

Server. A provider of services. When a message is sent to a class requesting a particular service, the class that sent the request is the client and the class that services the request is the server.

Solution domain. The targeted implementation hardware and software platform. For example, a solution domain could be concerned with implementing an application in Smalltalk under OS/2, running on a 386-based processor with 8 MB of memory and 60 MB of disk space.

State. The current value of the data objects held by a particular object. For example, a car may have a radio setting of 100.7 MHz, a gas tank value of five gallons, and a passenger list containing one object.

Static binding. Static binding, also known as *early binding*, associates a variable with an object class *at compile time*. This allows the system to decide what method to use, based on the type of object *declared* as being dealt with.

Structure chart. A diagram used in structured (function-oriented) methodologies to design the composition of the executables in the system, including calling sequences and parameters.

Subclass. A subclass is a more specialization of its superclass. It is related to the superclass by type (is-a relationship). For example, a *Car* may be a subclass of a *Vehicle*. Poor subclassing is sometimes used to gain function through inheritance, even though the classes are not related by type.

Subsystem. A group of classes that work together to provide a related group of functions. For example, an ATM application may have an interface subsystem that provides functions and classes related to communicating to and receiving inputs from the end user.

Superclass. A class at a higher level of abstraction. A more generalized, less specialized class. In the inheritance hierarchy, a class higher in the hierarchy from which state and behavior is inherited.

Test case. A series of messages to send, along with their expected results. The running of a test case typically logs the execution results. Test cases are used to verify that the system performs the functions listed in the requirements document.

Thrown away. Classes and methods that are created and deleted during a single application development (i.e., never shipped or kept in the company's class library) are "thrown away."

Total LOC. The number of source lines that contain active code in an application.

Total statements. The number of language statements in an application.

Total comment lines. The number of lines in an application that contain only comments.

UI. User Interface. This consists of the screen layouts and interactions between the system and the user.

UI object. An object that provides an interface between the end user and the system's model objects. For example, an ATM function menu window is a UI object for the ATM model object in a bank. The UI object classes change relatively frequently, as new technology, screen layouts, report formats, and usability studies require. They should be designed with low coupling with the model object classes, so that different UIs can be used with the same model object classes that are fundamental to the business.

Usability. The group that focuses on the ease of use of the application user interface. Also known as *human factors*.

Use case. A description of the system actions upon receipt of one type of user request. For example, an ATM application may have a use case for an account balance request.

Waterfall process. Development steps that develop an application by moving the entire set of end user functions through the phases as one monolithic set.

White box. Viewing the internal workings of something.

Index